The Survival Guide for
Newly Qualified Social Workers

of related interest

The Child's World
Assessing Children in Need
Edited by Jan Horwath
ISBN 978 1 84310 568 8
eISBN 978 0 85700 183 2

Practical Supervision
How to Become a Supervisor for the Helping Professions
Penny Henderson, Jim Holloway and Anthea Millar
ISBN 978 1 84905 442 3
eISBN 978 0 85700 918 0

Mindful Co-working
Be Confident, Happy and Productive in Your Working Relationships
Clark Baim
ISBN 978 1 84905 413 3
eISBN 978 0 85700 803 9

Mastering Communication in Social Work
From Understanding to Doing
Linda Gast and Martin Bailey
ISBN 978 1 84905 444 7
eISBN 978 0 85700 819 0

Mastering Approaches to Diversity in Social Work
Linda Gast and Anne Patmore
ISBN 978 1 84905 224 5
eISBN 978 0 85700 458 1

Mastering Social Work Supervision
Jane Wonnacott
ISBN 978 1 84905 177 4
eISBN 978 0 85700 403 1

Mastering Social Work Values and Ethics
Farrukh Akhtar
ISBN 978 1 84905 274 0
eISBN 978 0 85700 594 6

The Survival Guide for Newly Qualified Social Workers

Second Edition

Hitting the Ground Running

Helen Donnellan and Gordon Jack

Jessica Kingsley *Publishers*
London and Philadelphia

Table 2.1 on page 52 is reproduced with kind permission of Blackwell. Figure 5.1 on page 99 is reproduced with kind permission of the National Children's Bureau.

First published in 2009 as The Survival Guide for Newly Qualified Child and Family Social Workers: Hitting the Ground Running
This second edition published in 2015 with a revised title
by Jessica Kingsley Publishers
73 Collier Street
London N1 9BE, UK
and
400 Market Street, Suite 400
Philadelphia, PA 19106, USA

www.jkp.com

Front cover image source: Thinkstock®. The cover image is for illustrative purposes only, and any person featuring is a model.

Library of Congress Cataloging in Publication Data
Donnellan, Helen.
[Survival guide for newly qualified child and family social workers]
The survival guide for newly qualified social workers : hitting the ground running / Helen Donnellan and
Gordon Jack. -- [Second edition].
pages cm
Revision of the authors' The survival guide for newly qualified child and family social workers.
Includes bibliographical references and index.
ISBN 978-1-84905-533-8 (alk. paper)
1. Social work with children. 2. Family social work. 3. Social service. I. Jack, Gordon. II. Title.
HV713.D66 2015
361.30941--dc23
2014016303

British Library Cataloguing in Publication Data
A CIP catalogue record for this book is available from the British Library

ISBN 978 1 84905 533 8
eISBN 978 0 85700 955 5

Printed and bound in Great Britain

Contents

Figures

Tables

Boxes

Acknowledgements

Extracts from questionnaires and interviews with the social workers who have taken part in our research studies appear regularly throughout the text, highlighting many of the key themes which have emerged. We are extremely grateful to all of the participants who gave so freely of their time and who shared with such openness and honesty their experiences of working on the frontline.

Preface

Who is this book for?

As the book is intended as an introduction to social work for new entrants to the profession, it will be of interest not only to newly qualified social workers (NQSWs), but also to students in the final year of their qualifying programmes, the managers and supervisors of NQSWs, and training and staff development personnel responsible for formal programmes of early support for NQSWs, such as the Assessed and Supported Year in Employment (ASYE) in England.

New entrants to the social work profession

This book aims primarily to provide advice and guidance for NQSWs taking up their first post in any setting in the UK. It is designed to ease the transition from student social worker to qualified professional by providing the practical guidance and support needed in the first year or two in post. It gives attention to the requirements for formal NQSW programmes and the frameworks which underpin continuing professional development across the UK.

Final year social work students

The impetus for this book came from the development of new qualifying and post-qualifying frameworks for the social work profession across the UK. Qualifying students now spend a significant proportion of their education and training on placement, in a variety of workplaces, so it is helpful to know how organisations operate and what to expect in looking ahead to their first social work post after qualifying. This book provides a helpful overview of the rewards and pitfalls of the all-important transition from student to employee.

Managers and supervisors of NQSWs

Much of the advice and guidance in this book is based on the development of best practice. An effective social worker will be one who recognises the benefits of ongoing learning and seeks out opportunities to reflect on their practice. This book therefore offers those who supervise and manage NQSWs an opportunity to reflect on a number of questions and key issues which typically arise for new entrants to the profession so as to evaluate the ideas and methods they currently use in order to improve their own practice.

Training and staff development personnel, and ASYE coordinators

Professional codes of practice place a duty on organisations that employ social workers to promote their continuing professional development. This book can therefore be used as a reference for trainers, mentors, supervisors, course leaders and others who have a role in supporting, developing or monitoring the progress of NQSWs. It will also help those in training and staff development units to make some of the links between qualifying programmes and their workplaces in the delivery of formal NQSW programmes, such as the ASYE in England.

How is the book organised?

There are four parts in this book, arranged chronologically, which mark out progressive milestones along the route from the initial '*thud!*' of professional status as NQSWs 'hit the ground' and start running, then warming to the task, jumping the hurdles and making their way safely to the finishing line at the end of the first year or two in practice, better prepared for the next lap.

The chapters in each part gather together topics relevant to that particular staging post of professional development. Some issues, for example, orientation, are relevant at one specific point in time and are covered in depth in one part only. Others, such as supervision, coping and support, have been integrated into more than one part, to reflect the changing needs and thinking of NQSWs as they move through induction and beyond.

Each part concludes with an 'Additional Resources' section, signposting readers to useful sources of the most up-to-date tools and guidance for practice in each of the four UK countries.

Part I: *Thud!* Professional Status

Throughout Part I, we focus on the first few weeks of welcome, introduction and orientation to NQSWs, and aim to ease the transition into the workplace in these very early career stages. The change from student to employee, the development of a professional orientation, workplace motivators, continuing professional development frameworks and formal NQSW programmes are primary considerations at this time.

Part II: Warming Up

In Part II we move on from early orientation to consider some of the priority issues which present themselves during the next few months. Our focus now is on the more formal corporate and role-specific induction processes used by employing agencies, with more about time management and planning for continuing professional development.

Part III: Jumping the Hurdles

This part focuses on the period after induction, as NQSWs take on an increasing workload and begin to deal with some of the stresses as well as the satisfactions of the job. We explore ways of finding support from a wide range of sources, including a specific focus on a two-way 'supervisory alliance'.

Part IV: Going the Distance

As day-to-day practice becomes more streamlined and NQSWs begin to deal more confidently with the range of tasks allocated to them, this final part of the book considers positive coping strategies for working with increasingly complex and stressful situations, as well as the influence of the organisation on social workers and, conversely, how they can begin to have an influence on the organisation.

How to use this book

Some readers may choose to read the book from cover to cover, methodically working their way from front to back, while others may prefer to dip in and out when particular information is needed. The layout of the book makes it readily accessible to either approach.

However readers choose to use it, the book will provide practical guidance and advice about how to approach the duties, roles and responsibilities most relevant to NQSWs, including:

- managing the transition into the workplace and what's expected of NQSWs

- accountability, and balancing care and control elements of the job

- working within agency policies and procedures

- coping with stress and finding support

- making the most of supervision

- planning for continuing professional development.

Throughout the book a range of practice situations which are likely to be encountered in the early stages of practising as an NQSW are considered, with suggestions provided about how to deal with them. However, it is important to stress that these suggestions are not set in stone, nor do they offer a universal blueprint for effective practice. Rather, they will need to be adapted to suit the particular circumstances and preferences of the NQSW.

The Contexts for Social Work Practice across the UK

A common experience which has emerged consistently from our research with NQSWs is that many feel inadequately guided and supported, too often left to make it up as they go along, sinking or swimming as the case may be. This book is intended to rectify that situation, helping you to successfully bridge the gap between qualification and established professional, providing a route map to support and guide you through this transitional phase by:

- considering how knowledge and skills continue to be acquired and applied in the workplace as part of the development of professional practice and expertise

- discussing the duties and responsibilities you have as a social worker and how these are managed in organisations

- exploring ways of handling situations (with colleagues, managers and other professionals, as well as with service users) which may be new and challenging for you

- providing a range of strategies for managing yourself, your time and your workload

- offering suggestions for finding support, coping with stress and maintaining job satisfaction, and

- providing an independent source of support which you can use alongside any formal NQSW programme for which you may be registered during your first year or two in post.

Social work is a professional activity which is governed not only by formal regulations and requirements, but also by political influences and public expectations. This means that, throughout its history, social work has been a *contested* activity, shaped by the social, political and economic conditions of the times. This introduction is designed to provide you with a brief summary of the key contexts which currently influence social work practice in each of the four UK countries.

Public sector reform
The challenge laid down by successive governments for all public services, throughout the UK, has been to offer greater choice and control to the people who use those services, delivering them as near to service users' homes as possible and tailored closely to their individual needs. On the one hand, this approach to the personalisation of services can be understood as an attempt to develop more responsive and empowering ways of meeting people's needs with a focus on prevention and early intervention, while on the other it may be construed as a surreptitious way of shifting responsibility from government on to individuals and their families; the attractions of this are clear within the context of cost-cutting and austerity which have characterised much policy-making in the early part of the twenty-first century in the UK and elsewhere.

Devolution
Devolution was a key political priority of the New Labour governments of 1997–2010, whereby they sought to introduce their programme of public service reform across the UK. Following referenda in Wales, Scotland and Northern Ireland, devolved government began in 1999 and has provided the four UK nations with greater autonomy and increasing opportunities to develop different approaches to the delivery of services. Personal social services, along with health, education and housing are among the key areas of responsibility currently devolved to the four UK countries, yet overarching policy

on the economy, taxation and welfare benefits is still decided centrally by the government at Westminster.

All four countries have distinctive contexts, histories and cultures, established long before devolution, so that, as each attempts to address the political, social and economic challenges of the twenty-first century, it is likely that an increasingly diverse range of approaches will emerge, although to date there is arguably less divergence than might have been expected (Dickens 2012). On the one hand, differential policy-making offers opportunities for innovation and experimentation, with new and successful approaches developed in one part of the UK capable of being adapted and adopted elsewhere. One example of this is the appointment of a Children's Commissioner pioneered in Wales and now adopted across the rest of the UK. On the other hand, greater policy divergence raises questions about UK-wide citizenship, rights and entitlements to services, often reflected in phrases like 'the north-south divide' and 'a postcode lottery'. While there may be support for developing local solutions and bringing power 'closer to the people', divergent policies in key areas, for example the abolition of university tuition fees and the introduction of free long-term care for elderly people in Scotland, and free medical prescriptions in Wales, have given rise to growing concerns about the degree to which policy differences within the UK are acceptable or not, and what the implications might be for continuing levels of national solidarity into the future (Lodge and Schmuecker 2012).

The health and social care agenda

Across the UK there is consensus that health and social care services need to be more closely integrated in order to increase the efficiency of the acute health sector mainly provided in hospitals, provide more care in community settings, with 'home as the hub', and enhance prevention and early intervention, particularly for children, young people and families in difficulties, and adults with long-term conditions or complex care needs. However, although broadly similar policy objectives can be said to exist across the UK, the contexts within which they are being implemented and the underlying philosophies driving change are somewhat different.

In Scotland, for example, the strategic direction of reforms has tended to follow a collaborative model, placing emphasis on collective ownership and development of services. It has been informed by extensive consultation, involving the public and frontline staff, about how services could be moved closer to people in their communities, how to speed up access to services, and how to improve the standard and quality of provision (Scottish Executive 2006a). Policy, which aims to centralise complex, high-end services in specialist centres, while moving services to meet less complex care needs from the acute sector into the community, has largely eschewed the market approach, allied to targets, which has been pursued more vigorously in England.

The approach to policy development in England, which is based on separating the purchasers of services from the organisations which provide them, has emphasised consumer choice. The development of a mixed economy of care, involving both private and public sector providers, has been promoted as the best way of driving up standards and producing efficient services which are more 'customer-centred'. There is also a renewed focus on health promotion, as well as moving provision from acute hospitals into the community wherever appropriate, as in Scotland. However, somewhat paradoxically, the management of these transitions may require rather more collaboration than competition between different agencies and organisations, especially in relation to chronic and complex or multiple, long-term conditions.

The philosophy underlying the Welsh Assembly's ten-year strategy for health and social care (Welsh Assembly Government 2007) is to transform the NHS from an illness-based model into a health-based model, attending to a range of social determinants of health, influenced by the comparatively high levels of social deprivation and associated poor health outcomes found across Wales. To achieve these aims, the strategy has drawn on the development of partnerships across the NHS, public health, local government and voluntary organisations.

Uniquely in the UK, Northern Ireland has had an integrated health and social care system since 1973, but, in the face of nearly three decades of deep political and social unrest, strategic developments have understandably tended to focus on stabilising and maintaining services rather than policy innovations and future planning, so that change here has tended to lag behind other parts of the UK. The Department of Health, Social Services and Public Safety is the single employer of all staff, with services commissioned by the Health and Social Care Board assisted by five regional commissioning groups. As in England, a purchaser/provider split has been maintained, and services are provided on a geographical basis by six Health and Social Care Trusts, each of which has its own staff and budget. There are interdisciplinary care teams, but the degree of integration varies, with mental health and learning disability services being the most fully integrated, while those for children, driven by a range of statutory duties, are the least.

The key difference in Northern Ireland is that there is one source of funding, one employer, one agency and one vision providing shared aims and objectives, thus avoiding many of the problems experienced in the rest of the UK. However, tensions have emerged as integration between health and social care is not a marriage of equal partners, with the result that the agenda is frequently dominated by health.

Social work reform

New Labour's approach to the modernisation of public services included social work, to which it often appeared to hold an ambivalent attitude. Indeed, it is here that the term 'social care' rather than 'social work' began to take hold, with its connotations of semi-skilled, routine work, obfuscating for more acceptable public consumption the complexity often involved in professional decision-making, particularly in relation to issues like care and control, empowerment and protection, support and safeguarding, and rights and responsibilities. The programme of reform aimed to raise standards through increased regulation, inspection and target-setting, greater involvement of the voluntary and private sectors in service provision, and a focus on multi-agency and interprofessional working.

Separate regulatory bodies for social work in the four UK countries were established in 2001 – the General Social Care Council (GSCC) in England; the Care Council for Wales, the Northern Ireland Social Care Council; and the Scottish Social Services Council – each with a similar remit to maintain a professional register of social workers, regulate social work education and training, and set national codes of practice. It is interesting to note that none of these bodies include 'social work' in their titles, although Scotland at least avoided any reference to 'social care'. In 2013, reform took a further step in England with the abolition of the GSCC and the transfer of responsibility for the regulation and registration of social workers to the Health and Care Professions Council (HCPC) which has sought wherever possible to align its requirements to those in place for the 14 other, generally health-related, professions for which it is responsible. Unlike the other three care councils, the HCPC does not register social work *students*. Responsibility for ensuring suitability for education and training, and for dealing with student conduct issues, has been transferred to education providers under a new England-wide suitability scheme (HCPC 2012a).

In England, the programme of social work reform, which aimed to raise public confidence and develop a well-supported profession, began in earnest in 2008 with the establishment of a Social Work Task Force, which went on to make 15 recommendations in its final report (SWTF 2009a). The Social Work Reform Board (SWRB) was subsequently established, with representation from employers, social workers, service users, carers, trade unions and educators, to implement the recommendations of the SWTF in a sector-led process. The SWRB produced two reports (SWRB 2010, 2012) from which a number of reforms emerged across the continuum of education and training, each of which has informed and influenced practice changes in different ways across the UK.

Social work education

Social work qualifications, which are transferable across the UK, are regulated and approved by the relevant care councils (see Table I.1 on pages 26–7 for a summary). In Wales and Northern Ireland, programmes are generic, with knowledge and skills drawn from the National Occupational Standards (Topss UK Partnership 2002) and Quality Assurance Agency Benchmark Statements for Social Work (QAA 2008). Within the Scottish Credit and Qualifications Framework (SCQF), Scotland has developed its own generic Standards in Social Work Education (Scottish Government 2003) alongside Key Capabilities in Child Care and Protection (Scottish Executive 2006b), to ensure that at the point of qualification all social workers, regardless of training background or employment setting, are aware of their roles and responsibilities in relation to children and young people. The commitment to evidencing development in work with vulnerable children and adults is reflected throughout the learning continuum adopted in Scotland, including registration and re-registration requirements for all social workers.

In England, the programme of reform has introduced Standards of Proficiency for Social Work (HCPC 2012b), expressed as competencies for assessment, setting out what social workers should know, understand and be able to do when they complete their qualifying education and training. At the same time, The College of Social Work (TCSW) has criticised the focus on competence and introduced a set of 'more rounded, holistic and developmental statements of capability' integrated into an overarching Professional Capabilities Framework (PCF), consisting of nine domains within which descriptors set out how capability is to be demonstrated at each of five career stages: initial qualification; newly qualified; social worker; senior practitioner; and advanced practitioner, practice educator or social work manager, described in a distinctive rainbow fan diagram.[1] Concerns have been raised (e.g. Croisdale-Appleby 2014; Taylor and Bogo 2013) about how these two potentially dissonant approaches may be able or not to resolve the inherent tension in 'making what's important assessable and making what's assessable important' (TCSW 2012).

Work is ongoing between HCPC and TCSW to map the competences and capabilities against each other. Currently, meeting the HCPC competency Standards of Proficiency for Social Work is mandatory for all qualifying programmes in England, while those which also meet the PCF capability statements may seek an additional, voluntary endorsement from TCSW.

1   Available online at www.tcsw.org.uk/pcf.aspx.

Table I.1 Summary of qualifying social work programmes across the UK

	Wales	Scotland	England	Northern Ireland
Initial qualification – programme requirements	NOS QAA Benchmark Statements for Social Work	Standards in Social Work Education (SiSWE) Key Capabilities in Child Care and Protection	Competencies (Mandatory) Standards of Proficiency for Social Work Capabilities (Voluntary) PCF Stage 1 Initial Qualification	NOS QAA Benchmark Statements for Social Work
	Involvement of employers, service users and carers in planning, design, delivery, assessment and recruitment to programmes			
Approval and regulation	Care Council for Wales (CCW) www.ccwales.org.uk	Scottish Social Services Council (SSSC) www.sssc.org.uk	Competencies Health and Care Professions Council (HCPC) www.hcpc-uk.org Capabilities The College of Social Work (TCSW) www.tcsw.org.uk	Northern Ireland Social Care Council (NISCC) www.niscc.info

Initial training – leading to registration *Academic programmes Generic routes*	3-year Undergraduate 2-year Masters	4-year Undergraduate 2-year Masters	3-year Undergraduate 2-year Masters	3-year Undergraduate 2-year Masters plus Assessed Year in Employment (AYE)
Initial qualification – leading to registration *Children's services only, employment-based routes, graduate entry, M level*	None	None	*Step Up to Social work:* including employer sponsorship *Frontline:* Programme sponsorship and optional final leadership qualification	None

Genericism versus specialism

The debate about whether social work should be taught, practised and organised according to generic or specialist principles dates back as far as the Seebohm Report in 1968, and has been reignited more recently by two government-funded, 'fast-track' routes to qualification, applicable only to work with children and families in England. *Step Up to Social Work*, in its third intake at the time of writing, and *Frontline*, modelled on the *Teach First* programmes in education, which commenced in 2014, both offer high calibre graduates and those seeking to change career substantial bursaries to support them through employer-led, work-based training routes to achieve professional registration, alongside a post-graduate diploma, within a period of 12–14 months. An independent, government-funded review of social work education has stressed the importance of equipping students for a long-term *career*, not just a first job, in social work, and warned against a profession built on 'know how' rather than 'know why' (Croisdale-Appleby 2014). Although some strengths were identified in an early evaluation of the *Step Up to Social Work* programme (Smith *et al.* 2013), the researchers stressed that further investigation of the impact of the additional funding provided to these programmes, and the longer term outcomes and career trajectories of successful trainees, will be needed before drawing any firm conclusions about their value.

A stronger voice for social work

The media, which has a significant influence on opinion across all parts of the UK, has generally been antagonistic towards the social work profession. Negative and often hostile portrayals of social workers have repeatedly been identified as a key source of stress by practitioners (e.g. the All Party Parliamentary Group on Social Work (APPG/BASW) Inquiry Report, 2014). In recent times, public and political mistrust of social work has reached new highs, partly as a result of media reporting of high profile child abuse tragedies, such as the deaths of Victoria Climbié and Peter Connolly. The storm of media and government criticism that followed these two tragedies led to the ordering of 'a root and branch' re-examination of social work systems and practices by the government of the day. Among a raft of recommendations, the SWTF called for the appointment of a chief social worker to ensure better representation of the profession within Whitehall, and the creation of an independent and strong organisation to represent and support social workers.

Both recommendations have been implemented in England, with separate chief social workers being appointed for children's and adult social work, and The College of Social Work (TCSW) being established. The role of the College is to uphold professional standards (including responsibility for the PCF), influence the media and policy makers, and enable members to keep up to date and share knowledge and practice dilemmas. Although it is still early days for the College, it is disappointing to note that of the 87,870 registered social workers in England, membership of the College had only reached just over 6000 in 2013. By way of comparison, the British Association of Social Workers, which covers all four UK countries and has been in existence since 1970, had just over 15,000 members in 2013. While there is potential richness in the diversity of groups representing professional views in social work, one of the enduring challenges now will be to develop a recognition within the profession that if it is to raise standards and reverse adverse public perceptions, there is an urgent need to establish a more unified and persuasive voice for the social work profession.

Thud! Professional Status

Throughout Part I, we focus on the first few weeks of welcome, introduction and orientation to your first post as a qualified social worker and aim to ease your transition into the workplace in these very early stages.

In Chapter 1 we consider the requirements for registration, post-registration training and learning (PRTL) and continuing professional development (CPD), as well as the introduction of formal NQSW programmes (e.g. ASYE in England) which now frame much of the early workplace learning and development for social workers in both adult and children's settings.

Initial workplace motivators and the development of professional expertise are primary considerations for Chapter 2, while the change from student to employee in Chapter 3 includes consideration of the 'reality shock' which frequently accompanies the '*thud!*' of acquiring professional status. It is commonly acknowledged that change is rarely achieved without some stress and anxiety, so our consideration of transitional change includes strategies, coping mechanisms and sources of support for the first few weeks in your new post. However, given the importance of maintaining your motivation and building job satisfaction for your longer term career, we return, in greater depth, to finding support and making best use of supervision in Part III – *Jumping the Hurdles*, and the negative consequences of stress together with positive coping mechanisms in Part IV – *Going the Distance.*

Chapter 1

Managing your Professional Development

- UK continuing professional development (CPD) frameworks
- Post-registration training and learning (PRTL)
- Formal NQSW programmes (e.g. ASYE and AYE)
- Forward planning
- Key considerations in understanding your professional pathway

It is widely recognised that the first year in employment is a critical period in your professional development, frequently characterised by a plethora of requirements to be demonstrated, evidenced, observed or assessed, in different ways and at different stages, as you move through the initial stages of your new career. It may be helpful to think of the various capabilities, standards and indicators involved in your continuing professional development as being broadly of three types, related to:

- *Employers:* job description, supervision arrangements, induction protocols, probation and appraisal systems.

- *Regulatory bodies:* registration and post-registration training and learning (PRTL).

- *Formal NQSW programmes:* involving regulators, employers and, sometimes, higher education institutions (e.g. ASYE in England and AYE in Northern Ireland).

In order to keep on top of what can otherwise appear to be a rather complex and confusing range of requirements and standards you are expected to meet as an NQSW, alongside the day-to-day demands of your new job, it is important to have somewhere to store evidence of your continuing professional development. This is why we recommend that you set up an (electronic or paper) CPD file from day one in your new job. This will be of enormous help in ensuring that you have, readily to hand, all of the records and evidence you might need in relation to each of the key areas of your CPD (represented in Figure 1.1), relating to the requirements of regulatory bodies (square boxes), employers (oval boxes), and formal NQSW programmes (dotted oval), all of which will exert a significant influence on your early development as an NQSW. Differences in the ways that continuing professional development (UK CPD frameworks), post-registration training and learning (PRTL) and formal NQSW programmes (e.g. ASYE/AYE) operate in each of the four UK countries are summarised later in this chapter and at other relevant points throughout the book.

Figure 1.1 Continuing professional development file

There is more about professional development planning in Chapter 5, but here the strengths and areas for further development identified at the end of your qualifying education and training should be used as the first entry in your CPD file.

The UK CPD frameworks

Although arrangements for the CPD of social workers in the four countries of the UK vary, all place a responsibility on employers to provide appropriate training and development opportunities, and on you, as an NQSW, to make the most of the learning opportunities available and to gather evidence of your progress. This is to be presented for different purposes, in different formats and at different stages of your career. At a personal level, the essential elements of your initial CPD should include:

- an individual development plan, linking your qualification outcomes and future learning needs to your job description, induction and probation (all to be discussed in supervision)

- access to development activities (which may include formal NQSW programmes, such as ASYE or AYE)

- forward planning for appraisal by your employer (which should be linked to your individual development plan)

- a record of learning and activities which provide evidence of your progression and development.

Despite substantial work over the last few years to develop and promote CPD, social workers, their managers and employers have often found it hard to find the time or resources to engage positively with what has frequently been perceived as the disparate structures, activities and awards on offer. As part of the move to improve practice and raise standards, attempts to provide more coherent and effective frameworks have emerged, linked to career pathways and progression routes, in an attempt to improve the motivation, job satisfaction and retention of frontline social work practitioners. Formal requirements for CPD may be defined in the codes of practice, regulatory requirements, professional practice standards, practice governance frameworks, capabilities frameworks and career structures which contextualise social work practice in each of the four UK nations, but some of the key aspects currently in place across the UK are summarised in Table 1.1.

Post-registration training and learning (PRTL)

Post-registration training and learning (PRTL) is a key condition for continued registration as a professional social worker, with each of the four UK countries having developed slightly different approaches to their specific requirements. Full details are available on the websites of each of the care councils involved, but a very short synopsis is given at the bottom of Table 1.1.

Registration rules specify that every social worker must take individual responsibility for keeping a record of the PRTL they have undertaken, and that failure to meet this condition may be treated as misconduct; as suggested earlier, creating a paper or electronic CPD file from day one can be very helpful. With a complete record readily to hand, supervision then provides a good opportunity for you to:

- discuss PRTL with your manager

- identify specific areas for your professional development, and

- identify the learning opportunities that your agency can provide or to which access can be facilitated for you.

The *type* of activities that will meet the requirements are not necessarily specified in detail by each care council, in recognition of the fact that social work takes place in a wide range of settings and contexts. However, you are expected to choose training, learning and development activities that you have undertaken which:

- benefit your current employment

- benefit your career progression

- benefit service users and carers, and

- make the most of the learning opportunities available to you as part of your wider professional development.

Table 1.1 Comparison of the UK CPD frameworks

	Wales	Scotland	England	Northern Ireland
CPD frameworks	Continuing Professional Education and Learning (CEPL)	Continuous Learning Framework (CLF)	Professional Capabilities Framework (PCF)	Northern Ireland Post Qualifying Framework (NIPQ)
National career pathways, progression routes and requirements	Year 1: NQSWs "Making the most of your 1st year – Guidance for NQSWs" A structured approach to induction, probation, appraisal and practice. Subsequent development supported through four formal programmes of accredited and assessed learning delivered through employer/ education provider partnerships. Year 2: Consolidation Programme	Year 1: NQSWs Evidence of consolidation within 12 months of entry to the professional register. 144 hours of activities to advance professional development including 30 hours specifically related to protection of both children and adults. Year 2 and beyond: No specified timescales for progression but links between SCQF and CLF to assist in individual pathway planning, relevant to job role and evidencing CLF requirements in four key areas.	Year 1/2: NQSWs PCF Career Stage 2 ASYE programmes delivered through employer-led partnerships. Subsequent development through individual, flexible pathways evidencing PCF capabilities at five career stages across nine domains of knowledge, skills and values.	Year 1/2: NQSWs Assessed Year in Employment (AYE) Conditional registration with NISCC removed after successful completion of AYE notified by employer. Year 2 and beyond: Three types of PQ award at Master's level: Specific Specialist Leadership & Strategic

cont.

	Wales	Scotland	England	Northern Ireland
	Year 3: Experienced Practitioner Programme Year 3+: Senior Practitioner Programme Year 5+: Consultant Practitioner or Team Manager Programme	The CLF introduces personal and organisational capabilities to be demonstrated at four stages of progression: engaged, established, accomplished and exemplary.	PCF Career Stage 3: Social Worker PCF Career Stage 4: Senior Practitioner PCF Career Stage 5: Advanced Practitioner or Practice Educator or Team Manager	Flexible routes including taught modular programmes as well as individual assessment routes. Accredited courses delivered through formally approved and regulated university/employer partnerships.
Post-registration training and learning requirements (PRTL)	3-year renewal 90 hours of activities to advance professional development, recorded in a portfolio of evidence verified wherever possible by a line manager	3-year renewal 90 hours of activities At least 30 hours to focus on multi-professional working, assessing/managing risk to vulnerable groups. Evidence submitted via Record of Achievement pro-forma.	2-year renewal Meeting Standards of Continuing Professional Development No set number of hours. A record of achievement showing benefits from a range of activities to individual practice and to service users.	3-year renewal 90 hours of activity relevant to current or future practice

PRTL can be achieved through any combination of the following three different modes of learning:

- *Informal learning and practice development:* Although by no means an exhaustive list, you might draw on: reading, including government policy information, journal articles, newspapers and online publications; secondment or shadowing the work of a colleague in a related team or profession; undertaking a piece of research related to an issue raised in your practice; learning from reflection on a particular case or activity; taking on new or challenging tasks or responsibilities; and, giving a presentation, leading a discussion or running a seminar or group.

- *Unassessed courses and training:* These are more formal sessions, probably taking you away from the workplace, including in-house training (e.g. Mental Health Act assessments; child protection; adult safeguarding).

- *Certificated and assessed learning, through a higher education institution:* Although these courses of study may be increasingly delivered by distance learning or a blend of web-based and attendance days, this will generally be much more like the formal study that you experienced as a full-time student. It will carry academic credits and lead to a named award. However, to fit within a professional development framework, there will always be a focus on the assessment of your professional practice through written evidence to provide evidence of your capability, and a variety of observations and reports of practice from others – social workers, other professionals with whom you work, and increasingly those who use services and their carers, to confirm performance.

It is really important to take on board that CPD and PRTL are not necessarily about 'going away' to do a course of study provided by an academic institution. The three modes above emphasise that learning can take place as a result of almost anything that you do, in a wide variety of settings, situations and circumstances, and the trick is to remain alive to what influences your practice and to record the changes you make or the ideas that are consolidated and strengthened, as part of your normal routine, and which have become integrated into your everyday practice. This is where a reflexive journal (Chapter 4), kept within your CPD file, really comes into its own. Adopting this approach should also help you to discover positive connections between your own practice, that of the team, and the culture and strategies of the organisation.

Formal NQSW programmes

Each of the four UK regulatory councils is responsible for its own training requirements and guidance about how NQSWs should be supported and assessed in the early stages of their career development.

England

In England, the introduction of Assessed and Supported Year in Employment (ASYE) programmes, for all NQSWs in all settings – including the voluntary, private and independent sectors – from 2013 onwards, is one of the most significant changes to education and training in recent times. Nationally agreed protocols for the 12-month duration of ASYE programmes involve an initial reduction in the normal workload of a social worker in that setting (reviewed throughout the year), enhanced frequency of supervision and reflection on progress, opportunities for observing the practice of colleagues and other professionals, and additional regular peer-support groups facilitated by a named coordinator away from the usual office base. Assessment is intended to be holistic, assessing the broad spectrum of knowledge and skills in an integrated way, using the capability statements of the PCF at ASYE level to provide some sector-wide consistency. However, there is some flexibility, and programmes are implemented in different ways by different employers across the country.

Your level of capability will depend on your ability to manage risk, complexity, ambiguity and autonomous decision-making with confidence and professional leadership. Using the level descriptors within the PCF, by the end of an ASYE programme NQSWs should have:

Consistently demonstrated practice in a wider range of tasks and roles, and have become more effective in their interventions, thus building their own confidence and earning the confidence of others. They will have more experience and skills in relation to a particular setting and user group and have demonstrated the ability to work effectively on more complex situations. They will seek support in supervision appropriately, while starting to exercise initiative and evaluate their own practice. (TCSW 2010, p.19)

Although implemented in 2009 for NQSWs in children's services, these arrangements were only made available for adult services staff from 2013. It is therefore early days. However, in our recent research in which some participants had experience of ASYE, a number of positive benefits appeared to be emerging. For example, particular value was placed on individual coordinators and the ways in which they were able to act as an additional sounding board to resolve some early 'agency requirements-versus-personal values' tensions and dilemmas which had arisen, as well as on the regular off-site peer-support groups, drawing together staff from across settings and teams within and between agencies and focusing on early professional development for NQSWs. However, the ASYE only lasts for 12 months, and there is no similar national agreement, at the time of writing, about structured CPD pathways beyond these very early days of professional development, so that progression may remain an ad hoc journey for the majority of social workers, underlining the importance of taking control of your own CPD.

Interestingly, despite national agreements on the content of ASYE training, it is not mandatory for employers to provide it nor for social workers to undertake it, although NQSWs are *expected* to register for an ASYE within two years of qualification and (for most full-time staff) to complete it within 12 months. Specific government funding is available for agencies to support programme delivery. Importantly, assessment and decisions about the consequences for unsuccessful staff are the responsibility of each individual sponsoring agency, since there is no direct link with HCPC registration or re-registration. However, ASYE outcomes are clearly linked to the second stage of career progression defined within each of the nine domains of the PCF, and where candidates notify The College of

Social Work of successful completion, an ASYE certificate will be issued and a register of successful candidates maintained. However, any relationship between the ASYE, pay and progression currently remains a matter for individual agreement between social workers and their employers. These issues may be an important area to research when you are considering a new post or changing employer at any stage in your career.

Northern Ireland

In Northern Ireland, completion of an Assessed Year in Employment (AYE) has been mandatory for all NQSWs since 2006, with updated requirements issued by the Social Care Council in 2010 (NISCC 2010). The programme serves as an induction for NQSWs to the NISCC registration standards. Conditional registration is granted immediately to new social work graduates by NISCC, which is removed only on confirmation by an employer of successful completion of the AYE. NQSWs have professional supervision fortnightly for the first six months and monthly thereafter, and must undertake a minimum of ten development days in their first year in employment after qualification. Progress is reviewed throughout, with a final appraisal against the same six key roles for social work that apply to the qualifying degree, normally scheduled to take place no later than 11 months after first registration. A recent report (NISCC 2013) confirmed stakeholders' general satisfaction with the AYE scheme, but highlighted the challenges presented by a lack of suitable, permanent posts within which NQSWs could fulfil the AYE requirements.

Scotland

In Scotland there is no formal NQSW programme. PRTL arrangements are used to make a direct link between graduation, formal entry to the professional register and continued registration after the first 12 months. In order to ensure that all NQSWs undertake training and learning to assist them to consolidate their skills, knowledge and values at the start of their career, and to assist them to contribute to the protection of both children and adults from harm, NQSWs are required by the Scottish Social Services Council to submit an individual portfolio of evidence of consolidation of their practice.

The requirements specify 24 days of activities to advance professional development, which must include five days specifically related to both the protection of children and adults, irrespective of the social worker's role or setting. Following successful re-registration at the end of the initial 12 months on the register, NQSWs must then complete a further ten days of PRTL in the remainder of the three-year registration period.

Wales

In Wales, a developing Continuing Professional Education and Learning (CPEL) framework is used to describe the minimum arrangements for the ongoing education and learning of social workers in order to progress on the national career pathway. The CPEL includes four formal programmes of learning (see Table 1.1, page 37) based on national requirements linked to specified career stages. It is important to note that here the first consolidation programme, which commenced in 2013, is employer-led and is designed to be undertaken during the *second* year of practice after qualification. To support NQSWs in the first year in employment, CCW has issued guidance for NQSWs and their employers (CCW 2008) setting out detailed expectations, based around a personal development plan, to identify areas in need of consolidation and development and providing for a structured approach to practice through induction, with opportunities to meet with other NQSWs, as well as probation and appraisal. Although the programme is a compulsory part of the registration process for social workers in Wales, there is no assessment.

Forward planning

Your line manager will be directly involved in almost every aspect of your CPD, from informal discussion to integration into a formal NQSW programme, supervision, probation and appraisal, ensuring that your individual aspirations are part of a structured plan which coordinates development activities across the needs of the whole team. If your absence from the workplace on CPD activities is not understood and supported by your team, you may inadvertently create resentment among colleagues who are expected to cover your duties when you are perceived to be 'away on a jolly'. We have found in our own research that practitioners can view training opportunities as a welcome break from the normal office pressures and workload, but that it can backfire if the proper cover arrangements have not been considered, agreed and confirmed by the line manager *before* the event takes place, as the following newly qualified social worker quickly discovered:

> But in doing the training, there's the other part of you that's worrying because all your work is building up. You know, when you come back off a week's course, there's 150 emails and everything has kicked off and everything is a concern... well, you're working later every night that week just to unravel it all. (NQSW)

Another aspect of training that can turn a potentially positive experience into a very negative one is lack of planning to meet the additional burdens of study, on top of what is probably already a busy and sometimes stressful job.

> Well yes, I did get my study day but there's an awful lot of work that needs to be done outside of that day.

> You have to do it in some of your own time... I spent two complete weekends in addition to my study days, you know where I was saying to my family 'Leave me alone! I need to get this assignment finished'. (Social workers)

However generous your employer's arrangements are, it is unrealistic to think that everything can be achieved in your normal working hours. Your CPD will certainly demand some of your personal time as well, as illustrated by the comments above from two social workers, and you will need to have considered all of the implications and made a realistic assessment of how you will manage the extra demands. It might also be helpful to have time for background reading and research, and generally preparing your workplace, before embarking on a particular course. Again, forward planning as part of a coherent pathway, rather than just grabbing whatever is available, should allow you to build this into your timetable.

In our research we have found that there is often no clear policy for attending training, and it is left very much to individuals to take the initiative to find out what and when training opportunities are available and how to access them. This is not in itself a bad thing, but there is obvious potential for the generation of competition and feelings of unfairness, which can quickly divide or undermine a team.

All of these potential difficulties and tensions can be avoided through good coordination of learning and training opportunities by your line manager. However, before leaving this area, it is worth noting that, in our own research, we have found that managers have often been offered little by way of formal post-qualifying training themselves, and therefore have a limited understanding of what is involved or what the benefits might be. Although managers are often willing to let people go on training, frequently there is little acknowledgement of achievement or interest in the experiences of staff, with only scant attention paid to providing subsequent opportunities for staff to try out their new skills, as the following comments illustrate:

> But with reference to encouraging their own personal development plan, well you know, it's more about people just rushing off to do it if and when they have to. (Line manager)

> I think a lot of managers see it [PQ study] as just another hurdle. They see it as another thing that is impinging on their workers' time. (NQSW)

> And I gave my manager a copy of my portfolio and a few months later I asked him have you read it and he said 'No, it's in my drawer. I feel awful but I just haven't had time'. (Social worker)

If you find yourself in an agency which does not yet fully embrace the principles of what is usually referred to as a learning culture, you will need to take a proactive stance to ensure that you initiate discussion of your CPD and PRTL at every appropriate opportunity, both individually and in tandem with team members, so that professional development remains high on the joint agenda.

The proliferation of schemes specifically aimed at supporting NQSWs is beginning to indicate a move away from the expectation by employers that recently qualified staff should be able to take on an immediate caseload similar to that of an experienced social worker, which one government-commissioned report has described as 'illogical, highly undesirable and unsafe' (Croisdale-Appleby 2014, p.70). Good induction, coupled with schemes like those outlined above, begin to offer NQSWs a degree of protection in terms of workload relief, support and supervision. However, there is some way still to go if the recommendation of the SWTF (2009a) for a post-registration year of assessed practice leading to a formal licence to practise is to be realised.

Key considerations for effectively managing your development pathway

- Keep on top of what can appear to be a confusing range of requirements and standards for NQSWs by setting up an electronic or paper CPD file in which to store evidence of your progression and development from day one in your new job.

- Your initial professional development and post-registration training and learning are likely to be most successful where you list the strengths and areas for further development identified at the end of your qualifying training as the first entry in your CPD file. You are thereby forming the foundation of a properly structured plan, making links with your job description, induction and probation, in discussion with your supervisor.

- Remember that your continuing professional development can be based on almost anything that you do, including informal learning and day-to-day practice developments, as well as learning through training courses or formal NQSW programmes such as ASYE or AYE. The trick is to remain alive to what influences your practice and to record in your CPD file the changes you make or the ideas that are consolidated and strengthened, as part of your normal routine, integrated into your everyday practice.

Chapter 2

Developing Professional Expertise

- Professional identify
- From novice to expert
- The apprenticeship model
- Key considerations in developing professional expertise

You will almost certainly have entered your new career with high expectations and with the motivation to become the best practitioner that you can be. Your qualifying education and training should have instilled in you a commitment to ongoing enquiry and professional development, as well as equipping you with the skills to examine assumptions and use evidence to develop your own independent, critical judgements. These are the foundations of practice which help to equip you to meet the challenges of complexity, uncertainty and unpredictability which characterise contemporary social work in the UK. But what is involved in moving forward from this point in your development towards becoming a fully established professional social worker? In attempting to answer this question, it is helpful to consider what we mean when we talk about a profession, and related concepts such as professional expertise.

Professional identity
While professions can be defined in a number of different ways, most people would agree that they all involve claims to expertise, based on

47

university-level specialist education and training, as well as official regulation. These characteristics mean that, to a greater or lesser extent, all professions exercise power and control, which promote positions of privilege, both socially and economically.

Issues of professional identity and concepts of the power derived from expertise have the potential to bring professionals into conflict – not only with one another, but also with those who use their services. However, the willingness of the social work profession to draw from a wide range of philosophies, ideas and methods, together with adherence to the principles of partnership working and anti-oppressive practice have, to some extent, set it against the collective power associated with other professions. While consideration of these issues in relation to social work is therefore rather complicated, this should not prevent you from recognising in others, as well as aspiring to develop yourself, the knowledge and skills that give rise to legitimate claims of professional expertise. At the start of your professional career as a qualified social worker, it might be helpful for you to build up your own resource list of people who have particular areas of knowledge or expertise, including those in other agencies or professions, to whom you can turn for guidance and advice about specific aspects of your work (see Box 2.1).

Box 2.1 Defining an 'expert'

Can you think of someone who you regard as an 'expert' social worker?

What contributes to your understanding of this person as an expert?

Here are some possible reasons for your judgement:

- Advanced theoretical or subject knowledge
- Many years of experience in a particular role or area of practice
- High level practice skills or analytical ability
- Valuable personal attributes

Personal motivation

Personal motivation has an important role to play in developing your professional identity and expertise. As the following extract from an interview with a newly qualified social worker shows, if money is your prime motivation, you're probably in the wrong job:

> The money is part of it. Of course it is. It's a job. But I wouldn't be doing it for the money I get paid if I didn't actually want to try and make a difference to people's lives, because I do. And that's the thing that holds me to the job, it's the people that I work with…the variety…the chance to try and make a difference, but recognising that the majority of the time, it's unlikely to. (Social worker, 12 months post-qualification)

The chance to 'make a difference' is one of the reasons most-frequently cited by participants in our own research for choosing social work as a career, and we will return to this issue a little later. Here, however, we are thinking about what will motivate and sustain you in the very early stages of your post-qualification employment. The exercise in Box 2.2 identifies four factors, frequently quoted by professionals as primary workplace motivators, for you to consider.

Box 2.2 Assessing your professional motivation

Using the scale of 1–10 for each factor, choose the number which best describes your current level of satisfaction for each motivator:

AUTONOMY

- I am developing skills and confidence to make my own critical judgements

  Not at all 1 2 3 4 5 6 7 8 9 10 Completely

CHALLENGE

- I feel encouraged to take on new work and to try different approaches

  Not at all 1 2 3 4 5 6 7 8 9 10 Completely

SUPPORT

- I feel supported in my personal and professional development

  Not at all 1 2 3 4 5 6 7 8 9 10 Completely

ACKNOWLEDGEMENT

- My role is clear and my work is recognised by the team and managers

  Not at all 1 2 3 4 5 6 7 8 9 10 Completely

Low scores in all four areas indicate perceptions of limited autonomy, challenge, support and recognition, suggesting that your practice resembles that of a 'constrained conformist', operating in a directed and reactive way. In these circumstances you may consider your role to be one in which expectations are limited to 'doing what you are told' and 'toeing the party line'. Part of settling in to any new profession will involve an understandable and entirely reasonable preoccupation with how to get along within the system and get the job done. In the present context of public services in the UK, in which increasingly draconian political attitudes towards autonomy across the professions are evident, with power drawn away from individuals and towards central government, there is a tendency among many social workers to behave as constrained conformists. In what has become a very litigious society, organisations as well as individuals can struggle to maintain their independence, becoming risk-averse to such an extent that autonomous professionalism is almost extinguished. The breaking-down of professional skills into smaller, simpler activities, which can be allocated to non-professional support staff, has also eroded and effectively de-skilled practitioners across the professions, from law and medicine to health and social work.

While all of this is undoubtedly true, the danger here lies in blaming others for the way that you practise social work, effectively allowing yourself to become a victim. It is therefore important to recognise that, whatever the external constraints under which you are practising, your own actions, attitude and approach to the job are also important. Consciously maintaining the stance of a 'proactive professional', with independent views based on your own knowledge, skills and values, will influence not only the way you are perceived by others, including colleagues and other professionals, as well as people who use social work services, but also, perhaps more importantly, how you perceive yourself.

From novice to expert

The overwhelming majority of NQSWs are actively committed to keeping their knowledge up to date, and are enthusiastic about extending and enhancing their skills, as evidenced by the following quotes from social workers:

> Personally, I like going on courses. I want to learn, I don't want to get rusty so I will put myself on courses. (Social worker)

> And I really value training. I've always done a lot of training in my time in social care, because there's a lot more that I don't know that I do know and any bit that I can find out is useful to me. (Social worker)

It is likely that your qualifying education and training will have encouraged a commitment to ongoing enquiry, examining assumptions – those of others as well as your own – and to questioning, analysing and arguing from evidence to develop your own independent critical judgements. These skills provide the foundations for the development of your own professional 'expertise'; but what processes are involved in translating the skills and knowledge that you have acquired from your training into professional expertise?

Knowing what and knowing how

Based on a study of adult learners drawn from a wide range of professions in which, like social workers, individual practitioners were required to deal with problems arising in unstructured and unpredictable situations, Dreyfus and Dreyfus (1986) divided the knowledge and skills required to develop professional expertise into two types:

1. Knowledge based on facts and rules – in which practitioners can say that they '*know what*'. You might think about this as technical knowledge.

2. Knowledge derived from practice experience – in which practitioners demonstrate that they '*know how*'. You might think about this as practical knowledge or skills.

They then went on to propose a staged model of the development of professional expertise, with five levels of skill, each consisting of four elements, as set out in Table 2.1.

Table 2.1 Stages of skills acquisition

Skill level	Types of rules for decision-making	Exercising judgement and prioritising information	Process of decision-making	Level of responsibility and involvement in the situation
1. Novice	Context-free	None	Analytical	Detached
2. Advanced beginner	Context-free and situational	None	Analytical	Detached
3. Competent	Context-free and situational	Chosen deliberation	Analytical	Detached understanding and deciding but involved in outcome
4. Proficient	Context-free and situational	Experienced	Analytical	Involved understanding Detached deciding
5. Expert	Context-free and situational	Experienced	Intuitive	Involved

Source: Dreyfus and Dreyfus (1986)

Context-free rules are those founded on the technical aspects ('know how') of knowledge, in which you learn to recognise a range of objective facts and features which are relevant regardless of context. As a 'novice' learner, at the start of your social work training, you are likely to have formulated a number of context-free rules, based on your personal biography and values and the methods and theories that you were first taught. Then, progressing through Stages 2 and 3, first of all as an 'advanced beginner' and then as a 'competent' practitioner, you are likely to have gradually begun to modify and adapt these rules in the light of your experiences in different situations, initially in practice learning settings, and more recently in the workplace. During these stages of development, some of your early, context-free rules may be jettisoned altogether, but those that are retained will be gradually amended, modified and adapted to become 'situational rules' founded on the second type of knowledge, identified earlier as 'know how' or practical knowledge.

There comes a point in this natural progression when the sheer number of 'rules' becomes overwhelming so that, at the 'competent' practitioner stage, which is probably where you are in your professional development at the present time, you begin to develop a hierarchical process of decision-making, ordering and prioritising particular elements and selecting a plan of action based on conscious decision-making processes. This is when you begin to realise that your job performance is becoming more streamlined. Later on, at the 'proficient' practitioner level, the process of conscious choice and deliberation begins to be replaced by a greater reliance on understanding and recognition of similar situations and patterns from previous experiences, but even at this stage you are still likely to be thinking in a more or less deliberate and analytical way about exactly what to do. It is only, finally, at the 'expert' stage, that all aspects of professional thinking and doing become fully integrated and more or less intuitive.

Taking these ideas a step further, Fook *et al.* (2000) undertook a study in Australia which tracked the professional development of social workers for a period of five years, from the beginning of their training through to the workplace as qualified employees. This study enabled them to construct a theory of the development of professional expertise, in which they identified movement across 11 dimensions, including knowledge, skills, values, context, reflexivity, flexibility and creativity, use of theory, and perspectives on professional identity. The progression suggested by Fook *et al.*, from novice to expert practitioner, is summarised in Table 2.2 (page 54).

Together, these models provide a useful framework for mapping the changes in your thinking which are likely to occur over time, as you take on more complex work, applying your own situational rules while also developing and understanding the processes for prioritising and organising plans for action, and recognising and using the repeating patterns in your own experiences which finally become intuitive responses.

Table 2.2 Expertise development

From novice:		To expert:
Using context-free rules	➡	Applying and developing own range of situational rules, with the ability to select and prioritise, using independent critical judgement; generating a range of options; recognising multiple viewpoints
Dealing with personal/ professional tensions; often a 'constrained conformist', concerned with interpreting legislation and its influence on job performance; vision limited to 'how to get along in the system and get the job done'	➡	Demonstrating broader values and commitment to the profession; using the ability to frame change as a challenge or opportunity; separating personal and professional; grounded yet transcendent
Knowledge and skills seen as domain-specific and focused on the individuals in a situation	➡	Knowledge used creatively and readily transferred across contexts; planning and action undertaken as a holistic exercise
Passive detachment; standing outside the decision-making process but beginning involvement in outcomes	➡	Acting reflexively; interested in both process and outcome
Outcome-oriented	➡	Process-oriented; risk-taking, creative and flexible
Drawing on pre-professional personal experiences	➡	Using an amalgam of knowledge to create own theory/knowledge, which is transferable and can be generalised across situations

Source: adapted from SCWRU (2008)

The important point is that these changes are liable to occur at different rates and at different times, and not necessarily in a linear fashion. In fact, while the majority of practitioners will become 'proficient', reaching Stage 4 in the Dreyfus and Dreyfus model, not all will necessarily reach Stage 5 – that of the 'expert'.

The apprenticeship model

For some employers and professional bodies, the development of social workers is understood primarily as a technical apprenticeship, with new workers being inducted into a prescribed body of knowledge and skills in which they are required to become proficient. This model, exemplified by 'fast track routes' to qualification, such as the *Frontline* or *Step Up to Social Work* programmes for child protection workers, and some of the formal NQSW programmes, typically involves a new entrant to the profession being supervised by a senior colleague charged with responsibility for ensuring that a clearly defined set of knowledge and skills is passed on. The notion of an apprenticeship also carries with it elements of organisational control, to ensure ongoing procedural correctness in the ways in which the knowledge and skills transmitted are taken up and used (Tickle 1994). An apprenticeship is deemed to have been successfully completed once the new entrant has become technically proficient, having been assessed as such against a set of standard performance criteria.

It is important to recognise, however, that some significant limitations arise if we restrict our understanding of professional development to the enhancement of technical skills and knowledge within an apprenticeship model. It will be clear from what has been said already that this model is best suited to meeting the need for the development of technical skills and knowledge applied in contexts which are well established and relatively stable. This means that it is often inadequate, on its own, for meeting the professional development needs of social workers operating within the rapidly changing, complex and uncertain contexts within which they typically work. What is called for, therefore, is a more holistic model of continuing professional development, which is explored in more detail in Chapter 5.

Key considerations in developing as a professional

- While recognising the external constraints under which you may be practising, understanding what motivates you as a social worker should help you to consciously maintain the stance of a proactive professional, developing independent views based on your own knowledge, skills and values.

- There are limitations to an apprenticeship model of induction, focusing solely on technical proficiency and procedural correctness. Ongoing learning and the accumulation of 'practice wisdom' must be sustained as central elements of your professional development.

- Throughout your career you will need to use questioning, debating, analysing and arguing from evidence as part of your developing professional expertise.

- Take responsibility for your own continuing professional development from day one. It is important to recognise that a lot of your learning will come through doing and that 'not knowing' is a necessary part of the process for everyone. Make full use of your status as a newly qualified social worker to ask for help, guidance and advice when you need it.

Chapter 3

Transitional Change

- The transition gap
- Reality shock
- Key considerations in bridging the transition gap

For most practitioners, the *'thud!'* of professional status heralds a sometimes bewildering period of change, with adjustments needed to come to terms with the tensions between initial expectations and the realities of actual social work practice. In this chapter we consider the processes involved in making the shift from student to employee, and we identify and explore a 'transition gap' through which all NQSWs in the early stages of their professional development must pass, almost as a rite of passage.

The transition from student to employee is likely to be one of the most challenging periods of change that you will ever be required to negotiate. The success of your 'socialisation' into the profession depends, among other factors, on your ability to maintain the perspectives which you brought with you to your first job, while adapting to the cultures and traditions that you find there.

The transition gap

Despite the evidence of well-established theories about the process of developing professional expertise discussed in Chapter 2, the transition from social work student to qualified professional, during the first year or two in employment, is something that is now becoming better recognised as a specific phase of development in social work, with the establishment of formal NQSW programmes designed specifically to help bridge this transition. While there are important differences in the contexts and perspectives of what might be termed the 'helping professions', such as teaching and nursing, almost without exception practitioners are united in feeling that their first period in employment in these professions represents a testing time in which feeling unprepared is almost inevitable. Our own research with NQSWs has revealed powerful feelings, likened to being thrown in at the deep end before having been taught how to swim, and we have become increasingly aware of the existence of a significant but largely unacknowledged gap between the expectations and experiences of students on their final placements, and the reality of practice in their first period of post-qualification employment. Recognising the existence of this gap is the first positive step in addressing the deficit and getting the help and support that you might need.

Moving from student to employee

What are the key differences that define the 'gap' between being a student and a qualified employee? One newly qualified social worker expressed his feelings as follows:

> Ultimately, as a student, you're not responsible...when you come back here qualified you're given a caseload, and that's the difference, you are responsible and the buck stops with you and that leaves a different feeling inside. (NQSW)

In leaving behind your student status, you will no longer:

- be answerable to the academic world of your tutors, teachers or the university

- have the ready support of a group of students, all facing similar problems together, and

- be finishing your placement in a few weeks' time.

In taking on qualified social worker status you will:

- have duties and responsibilities defined by the policies and procedures of your employer

- carry a corporate identity

- be carrying full case responsibility, and

- be personally accountable for your decisions and actions.

Taken together, these changes will doubtless create pressure on you to perform confidently and well, and the gap between your previously familiar student role and your new identity may well come into sharp focus. The world of science explains the phenomenon of change from one state to another through the laws of thermodynamics, in which transitions between the three states of matter – solid, liquid and gas – typically involve large amounts of energy. However, this energy is described as 'latent', meaning that it is normally hidden from view, much as it appears to be in the crucible of first employment, when practitioners attempt to make the transition from one state (student) to the next (qualified employee). At the present time, the energy involved in successfully making the leap across this transition gap is typically not fully recognised, although the increasing availability of formal NQSW programmes should begin to provide some of the additional support that you are likely to need.

Underpinning and overarching knowledge

The transition gap is characterised by the interaction between two different sorts of knowledge – 'overarching' and 'underpinning'. The first of these is derived largely from the academic components of your qualifying education and training programme, while the second mainly develops in your practice learning and employment settings (Nellis 2001). Both are essential to the development of competent professional practice, and bringing them together into an individually balanced equilibrium is one of the main tasks for a successful transition into any profession. We have taken these ideas a little further, representing the two strands of developing professional practice in Figure 3.1 (page 60).

The specific contribution of overarching knowledge is the 'graduateness' which, as a successful student, you will bring with you into the workplace. As well as subject-specific knowledge, graduateness incorporates the ability to take a wider view, to contemplate ideas, to tackle complexity, to separate fact from opinion, to analyse and draw reasoned conclusions, and perhaps above all to foster an inquiring and independent mind. The black line in

Figure 3.1 represents this university-related strand of knowledge, and we have presented it as a solid line during your qualifying training, in recognition of its dominance at that stage. It provides you with the subject-specific knowledge from which you will have begun to develop, among other things, your initial repertoire of context-free rules, considered earlier, as part of the decision-making processes which are tested and explored in your practice placements. At the same time, underpinning knowledge, in and of the agencies in which you have been on placement, is also developing. However, while you are a student, without full case responsibility and with close links to the university, the development of underpinning knowledge is more limited, so it has been presented as a dotted grey line in the diagram.

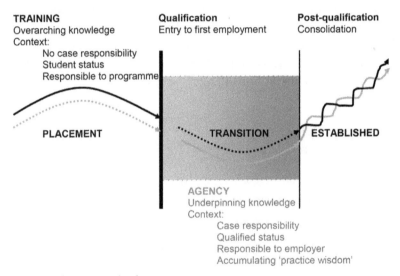

Figure 3.1 The transition 'gap'

The *'thud!'* with which qualified status arrives is indicated both by the thickness of the first vertical black line and the gap which follows in the development of both types of knowledge in the early stages of transition into first employment. This is very swiftly followed during the transition period by a switch in emphasis from the original dominance of overarching knowledge, now shown as a dotted black line, to prioritising the acquisition of underpinning knowledge within your employing agency, represented as a bold grey line. Now the context for the development of your learning is that you hold qualified status and full case responsibility, with your original ties to the university replaced by obligations to your employers.

It is only after the transition gap has been successfully traversed, and you begin to consolidate your practice as an established professional, that learning along both of these dimensions becomes more balanced and integrated. This is probably the point at which you will feel willing and able to take on more formal post-qualification studies, and will be looking to the CPD framework relevant to the country in which you are working to support your development through the next phase. This might be defined by the capabilities set out in Career Stage 3 (Social Worker) of the PCF in England, the Consolidation Programme of the CPEL in Wales, or modules at specialist level within the PQ framework in Northern Ireland.

You will no doubt have realised that these ideas resonate with the theories put forward by both Dreyfus and Dreyfus and Fook and colleagues discussed in Chapter 2. All of this evidence points to the realisation common to all new entrants to any profession that 'learning comes through doing'. The result is that, however well-prepared you might feel as you begin your first employment, the underpinning knowledge that is necessary for competent professional practice cannot be provided in advance of taking the plunge, and can only be properly integrated with overarching knowledge over a significant period of time. These theories and ideas of expertise and professionalism lead us to the recognition of a period of transitional change in the first year or two in employment, which is initially characterised by a gap through which all NQSWs must pass over before they can become established professionals.

Induction or probation?

It is also worth pointing out here that, although formal NQSW programmes, such as the ASYE in England, may make a contribution to bridging the 'transition gap', as they often draw heavily on an apprenticeship approach you will need to take a more or less self-directed approach to the processes of your overall *professional development*. Commonly, practitioners are effectively viewed as technicians, acquiring the knowledge and skills deemed necessary to do the job, the demonstration of which is monitored and assessed with a view to confirming appointment. While all of this is important, if you want your learning to be sustained as a central element of your CPD, it is essential that you make full use of what is available as part of any programme but also ensure that you are able to find other sources of advice and support.

Reality shock

As we have already noted, a bewildering level of change frequently accompanies the *'thud!'* of acquiring professional status. As far back as 1974 Kramer introduced the term 'reality shock' to characterise the adjustments needed as students came to the realisation that there was often tension between their professional expectations and the realities of the 'real world'. In Kramer's case it was nurses, but the shock is experienced to no lesser extent by new entrants to the social work profession, and the tensions between ideal and real practice can begin to manifest themselves almost immediately, as reflected in the following extracts from our own research:

Working to deadlines

The pressure from your line manager is more likely to be for the completion of reports according to a particular timescale, rather than the high-quality piece of considered writing that you will have been encouraged to produce for assessment as a student.

> Because I make time for report writing, other things have to go. I'm not going to hand in a poor quality piece of work... I'm not prepared to do that. (NQSW)

Individual accountability

Your primary focus in a case may be on caring for service users, but you will often be required to balance this with aspects of control, in which you have to take responsibility for unpopular decisions by the service users you are working with, and you will be disliked as a result.

It hasn't been easy over the last six months and I've realised what people, like, they really do hate you as well. You turn up and there's no way of sugar-coating what you've got to say and to work with people that absolutely detest the ground I walk on has been a real experience. (NQSW)

Working within agency policy and procedures

Sometimes you may go through the whole assessment process and come to a decision which is not then supported by your manager or the agency in quite the way you had expected.

I'm struggling with it at the moment if I'm honest. The reasons I came into social work are still very much there in my value base. I'm finding it conflicts with the position of the local authority. You know, I've got a case at the moment...I know the decision is about long-term budgeting, so it's kind of frustrating really that you are constrained by policy rather than good practice. (NQSW)

Tensions like these really stem from differences between the expectations you have of yourself, your concept of the value base of the profession, and your day-to-day experiences of work situations where budget management, performance targets and deadlines can all take on a greater priority. This is a hard nut to crack, but those who are able successfully to manage the duality of their role will have developed the ability to balance their personal involvement in people's lives with the ability to stand back, make judgements and reach often difficult decisions. Referring back to the model of expertise development discussed in Chapter 1, these abilities generally appear among the criteria attributed to 'expert' status, including such things as the 'ability to prioritise, use independent critical judgement, recognise multiple viewpoints, separate personal and professional, and apply a process orientation'. While they are unlikely, therefore, to be fully developed in the period immediately after qualification, an awareness of their developmental nature, and keeping in mind links to requirements of the CPD framework relevant to you, should help to frame your feelings positively, as part of the initial process of your socialisation into the social work profession.

Change and social strategies

Each one of the changes accompanying your transition from qualifying training into the workplace needs careful attention if you are to manage the process successfully. Social work is a complex and difficult job, and you should not expect the first 12–24 months to be easy. The ease with which you are able to move through the initial weeks and months in post, making adjustments and settling in to the workplace, will depend on a number of factors related to your own abilities, situation and circumstances, as well as what the organisation has to offer by way of support. We have represented this process of change, from one overlapping state to another, as you become socialised and established in the workplace, in Figure 3.2.

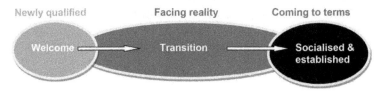

Figure 3.2 Professional socialisation

For some, transition is primarily a pragmatic step which can be taken at an early stage, exemplified by the following comment from one newly qualified social worker:

> Since it's not making me jump up and down any more, I guess I've grown up. I'm just going to work with what I have, keep a lid on and roll with it really. (Social worker, 12 months post-qualification)

Others may take longer, and look for more support in coming to terms with the changes that will be needed to help them feel at ease within the agency in which they are working. As we noted at the beginning of this chapter, the process of 'socialisation' will be strongly affected by the character, ethos and belief systems of others in your team and within the wider organisation. However, you do not have to consider professional socialisation as a *fait accompli*, in which you have no part to play and the organisation necessarily holds sway. It is better treated as a process of negotiation, in which individuals not only adjust to, but can also influence, the requirements and demands of their employers and the workplace. One useful model (Lacey 1977) suggests that there are three different strategies in this process, broadly described as:

- *Strategic compliance*: where, finding yourself in a culture which does not accord with your own values and beliefs, you simply comply with requirements which you may well feel are imposed upon you. This approach allows you to 'get along in the system', but does little to ease your integration into the team. Strategic compliance is most likely to be experienced in the very early stages of employment, as you first encounter some of the tensions between personal and professional expectations.

- *Internalised adjustment*: which occurs when you find you are in sympathy with the expectations and values of at least some of the members of your team or unit within the agency. Taking as many opportunities as possible to talk to and work alongside peers and colleagues will be very helpful to you in seeking out the kindred spirits that will help you to feel at ease within the organisation. The NQSW quoted above seems to have reached this stage of internalised adjustment after some 12 months in post.

- *Strategic redefinition*: in which you may attempt to introduce some new and creative elements into the workplace. The success or otherwise of this strategy will depend to a large extent on the ethos of the agency and its ability and willingness to respond to the changes proposed.

Adopting any one of these strategies, at an appropriate time, should help you to make sense of some of your emotional responses to the tensions between 'ideal' and 'real' practice, and how you are feeling about yourself, your colleagues and your agency, although other coping mechanisms will also be needed as you negotiate your way further into the profession and your workplace.

Coping

Coping is the means by which you maintain a sense of personal accomplishment and job satisfaction. Part III of the book focuses in detail on coping mechanisms, finding support and getting the most out of supervision, but coping is also part of the repertoire of skills that you will need when traversing the initial transition gap, and so one or two mechanisms are given an early mention here.

There is evidence (Stalker *et al.* 2007) that where those in caring professions are able to employ active, engaged coping mechanisms, they are more likely to maintain their sense of personal accomplishment, even though they might also be experiencing considerable stress. By contrast, using disengaged strategies has a negative effect on levels of satisfaction, and it is in this state that people may well resort to 'going off sick' as the only solution to the stress and emotional exhaustion they are experiencing. Examples of both engaged and disengaged mechanisms are listed in the following table:

Table 3.1 Coping mechanisms

Engaged	Disengaged
Problem-solving	Problem avoidance
Seeking social support	Social withdrawal
Expression of emotions	Wishful thinking
	Self-criticism

Your passage through the overlapping phases of professional socialisation (Table 3.1 above) will be most effectively managed if you are able to make full use of a range of engaged coping mechanisms.

In your own experiences of coping with difficult, challenging or stressful situations, what strategies and approaches have you called on to address the problems you faced (see Box 3.1)?

> ## Box 3.1 Reflecting on your own experiences of coping
>
> Think of a situation in which your own coping mechanisms have been tested.
>
> - Which, if any, of the criteria listed above (engaged/ disengaged) did you employ?
>
> - How well did you cope?
>
> - In what ways might you change your approach next time?

The principal message here is that no single resource is likely to meet all of your needs, and although some formal arrangements will be in place as part of your job description, for example supervision or regular learning sets and support groups, you will also need to be proactive and creative in seeking out and making use of a wider range of sources of help and support at different times, according to your own needs. These may include:

- making positive use of formal supervision

- seeking advice from your buddy or mentor

- calling on informal networks with colleagues and peers

- making use of family and friends

- contacting other NQSWs from your qualifying course

- enquiring about links with other newly qualified staff in the same building/team/locality, either for individual contact or to get together as a group

- finding out about and making use of any other support arrangements which are part of your formal NQSW programme (or probationary year).

Chapters 5, 8 and 9 scrutinise the issues of supervision, support and the role of managers in recognising transitional change and meeting the emotional needs of newly qualified staff.

Key considerations in bridging the 'transition gap'

- Learning comes through doing, in which time is needed to build experiences in a range of situations.

- However well prepared by education and training, the underpinning knowledge required in first employment cannot be provided in advance of 'taking the plunge'.

- The first year or two in practice after qualifying must be more than an apprenticeship, with a clear focus on: mentoring rather than monitoring; advice rather than assessment; and induction rather than probation.

- Prioritise attendance at NQSW support groups or learning sets (e.g. provided as part of a formal NQSW programme) or, where these are not available to you, enquiring about links with other NQSWs in the same building/team/locality, either for individual contact or to get together as a group.

Additional Resources

Regulatory body websites

Detailed country-specific requirements for registration; re-registration; PRTL from:

- Scottish Social Services Council: www.sssc.uk.com
- Northern Ireland Social Services Council: www.nissc.info
- Care Council for Wales: www.ccwales.org.uk
- Health and Care Professions Council: www.hcpc-uk.org.uk

England – guidance for ASYE

Capability descriptors at Level 3 within the PCF from The College of Social Work: https://www.tcsw.org.uk/uploadedFiles/TheCollege/_CollegeLibrary/Reform_resources/PCF10ASYELevel%20Capabilities.pdf.

Joint guidance, pro-formas and case studies

Topics include learning agreements; holistic assessment; direct observations; critical reflection; gathering feedback from service users; ASYE in independent and voluntary sector organisations from Skills for Care/Department for Education/The College of Social Work: www.skillsforcare.org.uk/Social-work/Assessed-and-Supported-Year-in-Employment/The-Assessed-and-Supported-Year-in-Employment-(ASYE).aspx.

Northern Ireland – Guidance for AYE

A summary of AYE guidance for NQSWs and employers from Northern Ireland Social Care Council: www.niscc.info/index.php/registrants/social-workers/assessed-year-in-employment.

Scotland – Guidance for PRTL

Guidance notes, NQSW PRTL Record of Achievement form and completed example: www.sssc.uk.com/Already-registered/post-registration-training-and-learning-prtl-for-newly-qualified-social-workers-nqsw.html.

Wales – Guidance for NQSWs

Making the most of the first year in practice – a guide for newly qualified social workers: www.ccwales.org.uk/consolidation-programme-for-newly qualified-social-workers.

Supporting Newly Qualified Social Workers in Wales – 2013 and beyond

Guidance on social workers' first year in practice for both social worker and employer from the Care Council for Wales: www.ccwales.org.uk/post-qualifying-training.

PART II

Warming Up

- Chapter 4 Getting started and what helps
- Chapter 5 Induction
- Chapter 6 Roles and tasks

In Part II our focus is on how to approach the first few days in your new professional role, together with the induction process within your agency, with more about managing your time and planning your professional development.

Chapter 4 begins by considering your preparations for day one, as well as the programme of basic introduction and orientation to your workplace, and concludes with some consideration of learning and reflection to anchor these two themes firmly at the beginning of your professional development.

We then move on from early orientation to consider some of the priority issues which will present themselves during the next few months. A key task at this stage, explored in Chapter 5, will be formulating a written supervision agreement with your line manager, setting out your respective roles and responsibilities, so that you establish a strong, trusting and supportive relationship. We return to wider aspects of supervision and support in Part III.

Learning and development are key themes integrated throughout this part of the book, as you move away from the information-gathering activities associated with initial orientation, and embark on your more formal programme of induction and support. Creating a professional development plan will help you to make the links between your qualification and previous experiences on the one hand, and your current work and future aspirations on the other. In Chapter 5 we suggest drawing on the capabilities and standards set out in the relevant UK CPD framework, at a level that is relevant to your post, as well as the requirements to be met within any formal NQSW programme on which you are registered, to gauge for yourself your growing confidence and the new learning needs emerging from your work role. We suggest a model for self-assessment that will help you to identify your strengths and turn any gaps into a range of learning objectives, helping you to create an initial professional development plan which you can use to inform decisions about the training and development events which you propose to attend over the coming months, as well as forming the basis for discussion with your supervisor about the types of work that you need to build into your caseload.

Chapter 6 moves on again to help you manage your initial expectations about roles and tasks, and some of the agency demands and bureaucratic burden, by focusing your attention on a 'hierarchy of needs', with good induction at the base of a triangle, providing the foundation on which you will be able to build your future development.

Chapter 4

Getting Started and What Helps

- Starting work in a new organisation

- Orientation

- Establishing a learning continuum

- Key considerations in getting started and what helps in the first few weeks in your new post

The first year in practice as a qualified professional is most commonly seen as a period of frenetic activity, in which there is a plethora of information and detail to take on board. Students emerging from a range of different professional training courses – social work, teaching, nursing – readily recognise that there is so much more to know than can be learned from a formal, taught course:

Nothing can prepare you for this job – ever. (NQSW)

Starting out in a new job is a daunting prospect for anyone, but it can be particularly so if you are taking up your first post in a new profession.

Starting work in a new organisation

Box 4.1 (page 74) suggests a number of points to help you reflect on your previous experiences of being a new worker. As an NQSW you may be starting work with a completely new employer or be familiar with the employer or workplace, either having been seconded through your qualifying education and training or having undertaken your final placement there. It might be thought that seconded workers would be in a better position to 'hit the ground running', but our research with NQSWs suggests that qualified professional status weighs no less heavily on their shoulders than on those who are facing their first day in a completely new organisation. In fact, if you are starting work following secondment, having previously worked in the organisation in an unqualified capacity, it is almost more important that you are able to establish yourself in your new *qualified* social worker role.

Box 4.1 Starting as a new worker

Think of a situation in which you were a new worker – perhaps the first day in the final placement of your qualifying training.

- How were you greeted and by whom?
- What equipment was ready for you on arrival?
- What was particularly welcoming?
- What was missing that would have improved your experience?

Welcome arrangements

On your first day, other than in exceptional circumstances, you should expect to be welcomed by your line manager and to meet your supervisor, if this is going to be someone different. They should be responsible for introducing you to everyone in your team, including senior managers and administrative and clerical staff, as well as your social work colleagues. More recently, some organisations have adopted the practice of identifying a particular person in the team to act as a buddy or mentor to a new member of staff, and it can be very helpful in the first few weeks to have someone else to whom you may turn for help, information and advice, in addition to your line manager and/or supervisor. This is a particularly effective arrangement because those providing your initial support are able to share the load, and you may feel more comfortable because you are not having to go to the same person all the time. Depending on where you are practising, there may also be an ASYE programme coordinator (or other member of the organisation's training department with responsibility for NQSWs) on whom to call for additional advice and support.

Whatever your route to qualified status has been, you will want to make a good start, and you will be aware of just how important first impressions can be in establishing yourself as a member of the team. As far as the organisation is concerned, preparations should begin well before you start work as a new employee. Criteria by which you might judge a good introduction could include some or all of the following best practice guidelines:

- preparation for your arrival which ensures you are expected by the whole team, including reception, clerical and administrative staff

- the presence of your manager and/or supervisor on the first day, to make personal introductions

- preparation of the team, including identifying someone to act as your buddy or mentor, to facilitate your settling in

- preparation of a programme of wider orientation, both within and beyond the immediate team or organisation, including visits and introductions to other teams and resources within your employing organisation, as well as key personnel in other organisations and the local area.

What will be available to you in terms of equipment, when you start your new job? It would be reasonable to be provided with some essential 'tools of the trade' on arrival, and you would normally expect to have the following:

- access to a desk – but bear in mind that in many offices a shared workstation or 'hot desk' is increasingly becoming the norm

- a telephone – make a note of the number and any extension

- a mobile telephone – make a note of the number and clarify the conditions, including private/personal use

- a desktop PC or laptop – with information about security arrangements and passwords

- a diary for appointments

- arrangements for car parking.

Once you have your letter of appointment, a quick call to your new line manager might be a good idea. In an ideal world, if you are completely new to the organisation, it would be sensible to arrange a visit to the team in advance of your starting date, to give you the chance, for example, to undertake the journey from home to work and find out about parking arrangements, get yourself orientated in the building, and find out how things generally work on a day-to-day basis, including what to expect on your first day. You could use this opportunity to ask about where you will be sitting and the equipment that will be available to you – so that even if the answer is 'not much', or 'don't know yet', at least you won't be harbouring false expectations, and any initial disappointment will have been avoided. Some of your queries might be about very basic information, like the arrangements for making hot and cold drinks and replenishing stationery, but often it is not knowing the answer to these more trivial matters that can make you feel a bit disorientated and insecure.

Box 4.2 Day one checklist

The following list suggests some of the things you might like to know about how your new office functions:

- What happens on the first day? Where should I report and at what time?

- Do I need a pass card or security number to get in and out of the building or into the car park?

- What time is the office usually open? If I need access to anything outside of normal working hours, can I get in?

- Where is the staff cloakroom and is there a secure place for my personal belongings?

- Is there a noticeboard or pigeonholes for messages and communications or is everything handled electronically?

- You might even need to know things like the 'dress code', or the arrangements for tea and coffee.

You will of course have your own list of questions to which you need answers, and even if you are not going to make a 'pre-appointment' visit, you should collect your thoughts together by creating your own checklist.

Orientation

For all new staff, a period of initial orientation will be absolutely essential to introduce you to your new surroundings. Good orientation may cover a number of elements, but we would suggest the following three areas for early attention: the people, the patch, and the paperwork.

The people

Take time in the first few days to get to know the names, contact details, job titles and particular areas of responsibility or expertise of each of your new colleagues. You should also try to include members of other teams, units or projects – noting names and contact details – with whom you will be liaising. Some of these will be social workers, but others will be from different professions, for example nursing, occupational health, psychiatry, psychology or education, and it will be a good investment to use some of the first few weeks in post getting to know the important players, and beginning to build your own network of local facilities and resources, both inside and outside your own organisation. Your manager may well suggest it, but you would be well advised in any case to make individual appointments to introduce yourself and to find out, first hand, how best to integrate into existing local networks and make the most useful links with your own role, so that when you are in the middle of a new piece of work and need to make use of a particular service, you will already have a good idea of what is available locally and, more importantly, you will already have a named contact.

The patch

This is about getting out and about to familiarise yourself with the geography, demography and general infrastructure of the area in which you will be working. If you are working somewhere which is entirely new to you, you will need to familiarise yourself with a wide range of local facilities, which could include buses and trains, hospitals, clinics, surgeries, day centres and refuges, residential and nursing homes, schools and colleges, job centres, family, youth and community centres, as well as whatever social, cultural, sport and leisure facilities exist within the locality. This is not an exhaustive list, but is intended as a trigger for the development of your own checklist, depending on your role. There is sometimes no substitute for pounding the pavements to develop a proper understanding of the neighbourhood and wider environment which form the context for the lives of residents in your locality, and to imprint some of the important features of the patch in your mind.

The paperwork

It's worth noting here that a study by Stalker and colleagues (2007) has shown that, although service users certainly provoke anxieties in all sorts of ways for NQSWs, this does not translate into quite the same feelings of stress, frustration and sometimes even anger that are experienced as a result of the competing pressures and demands of the procedural arrangements in their organisations.

> You spend all your time thinking about how you're going to get through this [IT] system and how to record it and make a square peg fit into a round hole. (NQSW)

> I didn't want to be a typist... I didn't train to do that. (NQSW)

> It's not that I haven't done the work, the work has been done, I just haven't got the time to write it all up every bloody day. (NQSW)

All organisations will have their own IT systems, documentation and forms, together with particular procedures for processing, approving and storing them. Unless you have undertaken qualification by secondment, or secured employment in the same organisation in which you have had a substantial practice placement as part of your qualifying course, all of this will be new to you and will certainly take time for you to operate confidently within.

Establishing a learning continuum

You might feel that your first year in practice is one in which your performance is endlessly monitored and assessed, and the plethora of requirements considered in Chapter 1 certainly indicates something of a testing time. With the support of your supervisor or line manager, you should try to ensure that the main emphasis is on your learning and development, rather than assessment. Some of the advice and guidance that will best support your professional development may be available within a formal NQSW programme, such as the ASYE in England, but we consider here two mechanisms that you could adopt yourself to contribute to the establishment of a learning continuum that will stand you in good stead far beyond the early stages of your career in social work.

Linking training achievements and workplace requirements

The standards for registration and re-registration as a professional social worker in all parts of the UK include a requirement to work on your own professional development. Qualifying programmes have generally assisted students to address this requirement for entry onto the register by providing graduates with a transcript and/or record of their achievement on the course. The document itself may have a range of titles and descriptions, specific to each particular programme, but somewhere towards the end of your final year you should have been provided with a summative statement, alongside your transcript of academic achievement, in which areas of particular strength and those requiring further development are identified, which provides you with the baseline for your initial professional development. Your achievement in relation to each of the standards and/or capability statements at qualifying level will also have been the basis for the assessment of your final practice placement. Because, by definition, the standards set out the general expectations which employers have of NQSWs, your own individual record of achievement provides you with an immediate link between what you already know and can do, and what will be expected of you in your first employment. These documents, identifying your strengths and areas for further development, should be among the first to be stored in the professional development file suggested in Chapter 1. You should ensure that you take the opportunity to provide your supervisor with a copy of your initial professional development plan, drawn from these documents, which should be used to inform your initial induction and continuing professional development within the agency. Ideally, line managers and staff development or training personnel, responsible for your welcome to the agency, should ask about your record of achievement and initial professional development plan, but even if it isn't requested, you should ensure that you produce it, and that you are ready to discuss its contents as early as possible in supervision. Used in this way, your evolving professional development plan is a key resource to assist you in:

- transferring baseline information about your present strengths and areas for improvement into the workplace

- providing a starting point for initial supervision discussions

- informing your initial induction and development programme in the agency, so that it is tailored as far as possible to meet your individual learning needs.

By actively using a professional development plan generated from your qualifying training programme in this way, you will have begun the process of professional development which is a fundamental part of your commitment to updating your knowledge and improving your skills as part of an ongoing, career-long process.

Keeping and using a reflexive journal
Your continuing professional development should also be closely related to your own reflections on your practice – how you think you are developing at the present time, as well as the directions in which you want to develop in the future. An ideal place to capture your thoughts and ideas is in a reflexive journal, which again can be conveniently stored in your professional development file. You may already have used a journal, diary or learning log in your qualifying

education and training, and you should not lose the habit just because you are no longer a student. The idea of a reflexive journal is to enable you to have a place in which to collect some of your thoughts and responses to situations or incidents that you encounter in your everyday practice. You might like to start the journal as soon as you take up your new post. You could begin with:

- an outline of your current role and responsibilities

- a 'skills and needs' analysis in relation to your learning – for example, skills you feel you have or wish to develop, and your professional development or other learning needs

- a self-assessment in relation to your knowledge and use of theory and research in practice.

As you progress through your first year and beyond, you will be able to revisit your earlier entries in order to evaluate any changes that have taken place. The aim of the journal itself is to allow you to reflect on issues related to your practice with service-users, colleagues or other professionals, as well as thoughts about your employing organisation, *as they occur*. It is important to remember that the primary focus should be on you, your thoughts and reactions, rather than on details of the situations themselves. You might find the headings in Box 4.3 (page 82) useful in designing a layout for your journal.

You could make use of a journal like this to meet the range of different requirements discussed in Chapter 1, as follows:

- to inform the agenda for supervision. Your reflections should provide you with some strong material to enable you to focus discussions with your supervisor directly on your practice – its delights as well as its difficulties.

- to contribute to evidence for agency purposes, for example as part of performance management and appraisal processes

- to contribute evidence to meet the requirements for formal NQSW programmes and assessment processes, and

- to contribute to regulation requirements, including re-registration and post-registration training and learning.

Box 4.3 A reflexive journal or learning log: format suggestion

KEY INTERACTIONS

- What happened?
- Who was involved?
- Where did it take place?
- What was the scale of the incident?

REFLECTION

- What issues did it raise?
- How did you use theories/knowledge/research/skills?
- What feelings were engendered and how did you manage?
- What tensions, conflicts and stresses emerged and how did you try to address them?
- What issues of difference, discrimination or inequality emerged and how did you work with them?

FUTURE ACTION

- What action might/will you take?
- What might you add to your action plan?
- What might you do differently?

Key considerations in getting started and what helps in the first few weeks in your new post

- Try not to expect too much of yourself – mistakes are an essential part of any learning process and everyone makes them.

- Try to frame agency processes and procedures, particularly those that are new to you, in a positive way. Approach the paperwork as a framework which can help you to structure your work so that it works for you – not the other way around.

- If you have navigated your way through a qualifying programme, you should have all the computer literacy skills you need to deal effectively and efficiently with your employer's IT system.

- Try to accept that reports don't all have to be perfect – good enough and on time is often a more realistic combination.

- Remember that you are not on your own and if you are in doubt, ask for advice.

Chapter 5

Induction

- Workplace culture
- Corporate induction
- Role-related induction
- Professional development planning

The section on initial orientation in the previous chapter separated out some of the early, short-term, information-gathering activities vital in the first few weeks to build your knowledge of local networks and resources. Induction processes are concerned with the way in which you are introduced to the more formal requirements of the agency, both as a corporate employee and in relation to the more specific duties and responsibilities of your role within the organisation. Induction in this sense will not be complete in the first few weeks in practice – it is more likely to be a programme of activities that will carry on throughout most of your first year in post.

Workplace culture

In the present context of public services across the UK, in which funding is often closely tied to meeting government performance targets, the workplace culture of many organisations employing social workers routinely prioritises operational efficiency and accountability over the well-being and professional development of their staff. In effect, this frequently means that the *quantity* of their activities and outputs is deemed to be more important that the *quality* of the work that they do. Of course, even in the present policy context there are exceptions to this general rule, exemplified by employers that recognise the value of nurturing and developing their staff, within the overall culture of what is often referred to as a learning organisation. It is in these organisations that you are likely to find the best arrangements for your induction as an NQSW. There is more on learning organisations in Chapter 12.

You can go some way towards assessing the strength of the learning culture in your own workplace by answering the questions in Box 5.1 relating to the arrangements for your induction.

Box 5.1 Understanding the learning culture of your workplace

- Does the agency have a written induction policy? Do I have a copy?

- Does my job description include NQSW support, professional development and post-registration training and learning?

- Is time allocated with my line manager for discussion of induction and development issues?

- Am I clear about which parts of the organisation (operational manager/staff development or training department/ASYE coordinator) can help in identifying my learning needs and opportunities to meet them?

- Am I encouraged to use my professional development plan effectively in relation to the requirements of my new post?

If the answer to any of these questions is 'no', it would be sensible to discuss the issue with your supervisor or line manager.

Where you assess your employer's commitment to professional development to be relatively weak, there are some positive early steps that you can take to establish your own 'learning culture', including:

- discussing your initial professional development plan in supervision

- seeking opportunities to try out knowledge and skills acquired from training in the new pieces of work allocated to you (in discussion with your line manager)

- linking the in-house training you attend to the areas for development identified in your professional development plan

- maintaining a reflexive journal from which you can extract issues for discussion in supervision, and use as a source of evidence for presentation within formal NQSW programmes, or as a contribution to your record for post-registration training and learning and re-registration purposes.

Corporate induction

Corporate induction programmes, particularly in large organisations such as local authorities, are commonly coordinated and delivered by the staff development or training unit, and will be set up according to a prescheduled timetable. Depending on when you start, there may be a programme for you to attend within the first few weeks, and this is certainly a good time to get a broader picture of the organisation as a whole, and of where you fit within its structures. Corporate induction will generally deal with issues that are common to all staff who are new to the organisation, and the topics normally covered are included in the checklist in Box 5.2.

As this checklist reveals, much of the content of corporate induction is limited to information-giving, and while it can be helpful to have this level of detail as early as possible, it might be quite a relief not to be asked to take on more information in the first few weeks at work, when you may already be feeling the effects of 'information overload'. There is a growing reliance on placing policies and procedures on web-based intranets which means, in principle at least, that documents are readily available for you to view at a time that is convenient. However, computer facilities are not always available to new staff in the first few weeks in post. Even when you have access to the system, you may still have to deal with the frustration of trying to locate a document that appears to be hidden deep within the organisation's intranet. It is a good idea, then, to use the corporate induction sessions to try to collect as many policies and procedure documents in paper format as you can, and to ensure that you are clear exactly where and how the various policies and procedures referred to in any sessions you attend can be accessed afterwards, perhaps to be stored in your professional development file, discussed in Chapter 1.

Box 5.2 Corporate induction: checklist

Although not exhaustive, the following list brings together the key elements that you should expect to find as part of any corporate induction programme.

- Organisational structure

- Mission statement – goals, values and priorities of the organisation

- Personnel policies – health and safety, annual leave, sickness and data protection

- Finance policies and procedures – pay, pension and travel; expenses

- Codes of conduct, grievance and disciplinary procedures

- Performance management and appraisal systems

Role-related induction

A properly structured programme of role-related induction, agreed in consultation with your manager, should include:

- recognition of areas of existing experience, knowledge and strength (which makes links with your professional development plan)

- a comprehensive list of people and places to visit (as already considered in Chapter 4)

- identification of documentation and literature to read (including handbooks and operating manuals, and examples of written work, such as case notes, assessment forms and court reports, to familiarise yourself with the style and standards that apply within the agency)

- a structure and timetable for the programme (that integrates corporate elements of induction with more role-specific requirements)

- arrangements for your registration and support on any formal NQSW programme, such as ASYE/AYE, including details of supervision, workload reduction and additional support through learning sets or peer group sessions.

As the following quotes illustrate, many agencies invest significant resources in their induction packages, including the provision of a range of training courses.

> I've worked for private companies and I cannot think of one company I've worked for who've invested the same kind of money that this local authority has invested in me... They've invested a huge amount. (NQSW)

> The agency are committed to it [PQ consolidation module], yes, they can do the financial bit, but in terms of all the other things, it's not there. (NQSW)

Unfortunately, as the second quote suggests, although formal NQSW programmes are gaining ground in many organisations, the additional support for newly qualified staff is still not always part of a coherent, overall workforce strategy. Where close links are not made between the delivery of high-quality services and the role-related and continuing professional development needs of staff, particularly NQSWs, much of the value of any initial investment in support schemes may be lost. Successful induction requires an active partnership between operational managers and staff-development personnel, as part of strategies to promote an overall learning culture in which there is good communication across all levels of the organisation.

In parallel with the corporate processes, role-specific induction for NQSWs should address the issues which are more closely related to your particular job and the expectations, duties and responsibilities of your qualified social worker role. It ought to be:

- coordinated with what is available at a more corporate level

- standardised across the agency, to cover activities during your first 12 months in post, and

- linked to your individual development plan, including learning opportunities and continuing professional development arrangements.

A structured induction programme

The checklist in Box 5.3, and the sections which follow it, provide a guide to the content of a well-planned, role-related induction programme.

Box 5.3 Role-related induction: checklist

You should expect your induction programme (discussed and agreed with your manager) to include the following:

- A named person responsible for your induction programme

- A reduced and protected caseload

- Good quality supervision that is regular and planned, defined in a formal policy document

- Consideration of re-registration requirements (PRTL) and codes of practice

- An organisational structure diagram

- Agency procedures manual(s)

- Individual development planning

A named person responsible for your agency induction programme

In some cases this task may be delegated to a member of the staff development or training unit, who may also be the NQSW/ASYE programme coordinator. This can be useful for making these wider connections in the early stages of your appointment; however, there really needs to be close involvement with your line manager and/or supervisor. It is vital that your line manager is aware of the content, pace and timetable of your induction programme so that, as well as monitoring and reviewing your progress, your workload can be tailored to your needs and built up around the development opportunities you have been offered. It is well recognised that learning is most effectively consolidated when you have a chance to try out in practice, as soon as possible after returning to your workplace, something new that you have learned as part of a training course, and your line manager will be best placed to provide this central link between induction activities and the work which is allocated to you. You can assist by ensuring that these links are reviewed and progressed in supervision.

A 'reduced and protected' workload

This should mean that responsibilities and allocated cases or other tasks are built up gradually, taking account of your previous experience and strengths, as well as the programme of learning and development agreed as part of your specific induction and any formal NQSW programme on which you are registered.

The best induction programmes will offer a case-free introductory period, in which you will be able to undertake orientation and information-gathering tasks, as well as spending time with your new team, allowing you to observe how things work on a day-to-day basis and to absorb something of the workplace culture. This introductory period might also provide opportunities for shadowing or co-working with more experienced social workers or other professionals, to increase your awareness of relevant legislation, protocols, procedures and processes in particular situations, and allowing you to observe some of the skills and knowledge being used by more experienced colleagues. An introductory period like this should also give you the opportunity to read through case notes, recordings, assessments and reports that others have produced, to help familiarise yourself with the structure, content and quality that is expected in written work for your agency.

Even if you don't have the luxury of a completely case-free introduction, it would be unusual now, as a newly qualified worker, not to have some reduction in the size of your workload for an initial period. In all probability, a reduced caseload will be defined using a range of criteria related to the team and setting in which you are working. Calculations may be simply numerical – for example, the number of people or families involved – or may take account of other factors, such as process stage, risk and complexity. Whichever caseload management system is used, you should ensure that you understand how your caseload has been worked out, and that you are clear about how any policy on reduction is going to be implemented (and brought to an end). Ideally, this should be a flexible process, reviewed and updated regularly in supervision discussions with your line manager, in the light of your own progress and how the work allocated to you is developing. Guidance relevant to this area has been offered in the detail of some formal NQSW programmes, which commonly specify that NQSWs should not be expected to take on the same level of responsibility as other social workers, and in their first year in post they should carry 90 per cent of the work that a confident second- or third-year social worker would be expected to undertake.

As well as some reduction in the size of your caseload in the early stages of your employment, protection from some *types of work* should also be arranged. It would be reasonable to expect that the level of work allocated to you in the first few weeks would be similar to the sort of work that you undertook as a final-year student. Protection will be particularly relevant in areas of work to which you were not exposed as a student, as emphasised in recent guidance from TCSW on the roles and functions of social workers, which states that NQSWs 'should not be expected to take responsibility alone for cases involving complex risk or high level of ambiguity – for example, cases that involve taking court/legal action, or deciding if a case meets the threshold for statutory intervention in safeguarding and child protection cases' (TCSW, 2014, p.19). Again, you need to ensure that you are clear about the policies that exist, and the ways in which they will be applied to you. Shadowing and co-working in these protected areas, with guidance and advice from more experienced colleagues, are good ways in which you can build up your knowledge and confidence in new areas of work.

Typically, formal NQSW programmes such as ASYE/AYE suggest that 10 per cent of an NQSW's time must be ring-fenced for professional development activities. For those working full-time, this equates to half a day each week in which you should have the freedom to pursue some aspect of your professional development – for instance attending courses, reading, researching, or attending peer-mentoring/support groups (see Box 5.4).

Box 5.4 A 'reduced and protected' workload: checklist
KEY AREAS FOR AGREEMENT WITH YOUR MANAGER

- Case-free introduction
- Reduced caseload (e.g. 90% of 'normal' caseload)
- Protected caseload (complexity and risk, building on your previous experience, stage of development and capability level identified in the UK CPD framework relevant to you)
- Protection of time (half day per week for professional development)
- Shadowing (to build knowledge and understanding in protected areas of practice)
- Co-working (to build confidence in more complex areas, without case responsibility)
- Changes to caseload linked to your professional development plan discussed in supervision

Supervision

There is little doubt that supervision is of paramount importance to all professionally qualified social workers, and Chapter 9 is dedicated entirely to this subject, but it is hardly possible to consider induction without giving some attention to the initial arrangements for your supervision. Good quality, planned supervision, which takes place on a regular basis, is an important learning and support mechanism at all stages of professional development and is increasingly recognised as such within formal NQSW programmes. As a student, you will already have experienced a variety of styles and approaches to supervision, but at that time you will also have had the support and guidance of a practice teacher, as well as course tutors and the student group of which you were a member.

To be effective, supervision needs to include consideration of *your* needs, not solely those of your employing organisation. All social workers, regardless of their experience, will have particular needs at different times, and you should avoid any tendency to regard supervision as a process only for dealing with problems. Access to supervision is your right as a professional worker, in accordance with the codes of practice implemented by each of the UK care councils, and you must be ready to take full advantage of the opportunities available to you. It will also be written into your contract of employment, and you should ensure that you are clear about its functions. Supervision is a process which should enable you to learn and grow, both personally and professionally, as well as supporting you in dealing with the stresses and pressures of the job. All agencies that employ qualified social workers should have a policy that defines supervision and clarifies expectations, and it is important that you familiarise yourself with it.

Several definitions of supervision exist, each identifying a range of aims and objectives which are explored in more detail in Chapter 9, but with brevity in mind for now, Table 5.1 provides a useful summary of the three main aspects.

Table 5.1 Supervision: summary of aims and functions

Aim	Function
To enable you to carry out your work effectively	Organisational/managerial
To develop your practice through lifelong learning and professional development	Professional/educational
To support and help you address the emotional pressures and stress of the work	Personal/interpersonal

In the early stages of your career you should expect to have more frequent supervision than will be available to you as a more established professional. As already discussed in Chapter 1, formal NQSW programmes like the ASYE in England stipulate that supervision for NQSWs should take place weekly for the first six weeks of employment, fortnightly for the next six months and monthly thereafter. It is also suggested that each session should last for an hour and a half of uninterrupted time.

Unfortunately, although common expectations about the *quantity* of supervision are becoming established across all four UK nations, variable reports of its *quality* remain and have certainly emerged from our own research. Supervision should be tailored to each person's stage of development, confidence and capabilities, the learning opportunities undertaken, and the range of work/level of responsibility held. The supervisor/supervisee relationship is an important one, and how you are going to work together will need to be established in a clear and unambiguous way. As pointed out by Morrison (2001), a written contract will have been the basis for your practice learning as a student, and there is no reason why your supervision as an NQSW should not take place within a similarly structured, written agreement. In the early stages of your professional development, clear structures, practical information and emotional support are all important elements in providing you with reassurance about your practice, and a supervisor who has a positive, tolerant and approachable style will be best placed to offer you effective help. As an NQSW you are likely to have a limited range of practice experience on which to draw, so that each piece of work may take you into unfamiliar territory, presenting new and sometimes perplexing challenges. As we saw in Chapter 2, these new experiences begin to become more manageable as you move from practice guided by context-free rules to the development of your own set of situational rules. The ability to see wider patterns in the work that you are undertaking will be developing, but in these early days you are likely to be dealing with each piece of work somewhat separately, focusing closely on the details of each new situation. Supervision should provide the time and support you need to be able to make the links between different cases and experiences, facilitating the process of ordering and prioritising particular elements.

As an NQSW at the start of your career, no doubt with high expectations of yourself, it is easy to become over-sensitised to any minor failings that may occur. In these circumstances, it is not unusual to find yourself overwhelmed by emotion at times, and supervision should help you to reflect on your expectations of yourself, ensuring that they are realistic. Remember to focus as much on what went right and was successful as on what may have gone wrong, using supervision to help you reframe any feelings of 'failure' as a natural part of your professional development. Learning from challenging situations will often remain indelibly etched on your memory, and it is from these experiences, with appropriate time for reflection and recovery through supervision, that the greatest practice improvements often occur.

More important than the document's format is that the supervision agreement should be arrived at through negotiation, with issues that are likely to arise and how they will be addressed and managed within the process clearly identified. There are many examples of written contracts for supervision, and if your agency has an overarching supervision policy this may include a preferred format. However, if you find that your employing agency does not provide any guidance, you might find the checklist in Box 5.5 helpful.

Box 5.5 Supervision agreement checklist

You may find the following suggestions helpful as headings for discussion with your line manager to develop a written agreement for supervision.

- Agenda setting – responsibilities and arrangements
- Frequency, duration and venue
- Permitted interruptions
- Method of recording
- Confidentiality – what is to remain confidential; what can be discussed elsewhere
- Expectations and contribution of supervisor and supervisee
- Use of individual development plan

- Arrangements for dealing with problems within supervision
- Date for review of the agreement
- Signatures of both parties

Re-registration and codes of practice

Re-registration requirements are clearly linked to your professional development plan and to the ongoing improvement of professional standards. Registration brought with it the '*thud!*' of first acquiring professional status that we considered in Part I, and the requirements for periodic re-registration could well arrive with a similar shock if you do not keep a written record of your learning and development. Establishing good habits from the very beginning will pay dividends a bit further down the line, and you should try to familiarise yourself with exactly what is required by the care council relevant to the country in which you are working. Post-registration training and learning (PRTL), which has already been considered in more detail in Chapter 1, is an essential part of re-registration and is the place where you are required to formally confirm your commitment to learning throughout your professional career. Each care council website provides online guidance, including examples of how to evidence the requirements in different formats, and larger employers are also likely to have recording systems, probably on their intranet, that will help you maintain an appropriate record of your ongoing learning and professional development activities. It would be a good idea to check out before you start what help might be available to you, but in the final analysis it is the individual responsibility of each professional social worker to maintain a PRTL record. Whatever the preferred or required format, the professional development file identified at the centre of Figure 1.1 in Chapter 1 (page 34) provides the central repository in which you can store, in one place, a record of texts and journals you have read; website and other online materials you have consulted; courses, conferences and seminars you have attended; and presentations you have made – to the team, other colleagues/ professionals, or service users and carers. Later on, some of the information which you have already collected for PRTL purposes will also feed directly into your professional development plan, as well as into evidence requirements for formal NQSW programmes and the agency's appraisal and performance management systems.

Over recent years, the regulatory bodies in the four UK countries have each developed codes of practice for social workers and their employers (See 'Additional Resources' at the end of Part II). Among other things, these codes require that social workers are personally accountable for the quality of their work. This means that you are under an obligation to tell your employer (and seek appropriate help) if you consider that you are not competent to perform any of the tasks that have been allocated to you. In addition, despite ongoing debate and concern about the relevance of private behaviour for social practice, and how far regulation should be allowed to intrude into the personal lives of social workers, it is also important to note here that 'fitness to practice' is concerned not only with conduct in the workplace, but also with any behaviour outside of work that affects public safety and the reputation of the profession. Annual reports including complaints made against social workers under their respective codes of conduct are published by the regulatory bodies. A recent review in England (GSCC 2013), for example, revealed that 81 per cent of complaints about conduct involved some aspect of 'unacceptable behaviour' in which there were particular issues around allegations of inappropriate relationships between social workers and people who use services. As an NQSW, it is crucial that you are careful to maintain appropriate, professional relationships at all times with people who use services. Concerns would arise if there are certain individuals or groups of service users for whom you take on extra things, and some for whom you don't. Are you setting up unfair expectations that other staff might have to cope with? Are you treating people with respect, dignity and fairness? What are your motives? A good indicator to guide your behaviour is never to do anything that you feel you could not tell your manager about. If you can't tell others what you are doing, then you probably shouldn't be doing it.

Organisational structure diagram

It is important that you are able to clearly identify your place and that of your team and your manager in relation to the wider organisation, and a structure diagram should help to clarify relevant line management and reporting responsibilities, both horizontally and vertically, through the various tiers of the organisation. As you become more established in the workplace, knowledge of organisational structures and processes is likely to have an increasingly important influence on your practice. Using such knowledge to promote best practice is an integral part of what might be termed the 'political' aspect of organisational life, and those who understand how organisations work will be well placed to achieve outcomes and promote changes for the benefit of service users and carers, as well as themselves and their colleagues.

Procedures manuals

Procedures manuals should help you to build your knowledge and understanding of the way in which the organisation functions and requires you to practise in key areas. Those detailing professional procedures should provide information about the framework for practice agreed within your employing agency. A well-produced manual will give you clear guidance about relevant areas of your work, providing information about the application of legislation and policy, assessment frameworks and thresholds, information-sharing protocols, decision-making processes and safe working practices, particularly in relation to lone working. There may also be separate manuals which provide guidance about the agency's various administrative processes, including the forms needed for each task. Frustration with bureaucracy can be avoided if you know what form is needed for a specific task, and where to look for it. It is advisable to get hold of written copies of any manuals used in your employing agency (in addition to web-based versions), since these are often lengthy documents which are not easy to digest on screen, and you may need to refer to them alongside other documents on your computer.

Professional development planning

Throughout this chapter we have referred to the centrality of learning in your professional development. Rather like the supervision agreement discussed earlier, a professional development plan requires periodic review and updating if it is to play an active role in guiding your continuing professional development. The planning process can be understood as a continuing cycle, as illustrated in Figure 5.1.

Figure 5.1 Professional development planning process
(reproduced from Noakes *et al.* 1998)

Self-assessment

The cyclical process suggested here begins with a self-assessment against the professional standards, competencies or capabilities set out in the UK CPD framework relevant to your post, which might also include any formal NQSW programme indicators and outcomes. The intention of this stage of the process is to help you to think about how your previous experience and learning match up with the demands of your new job. To do this, it is helpful to ask yourself three questions against *each* standard being considered:

- What knowledge, skills and values do I already have in this area?

- What do I need to learn to address any gaps?

- How am I going to learn the new things I have identified?

You might find it helpful to record your self-assessment in tabular form, as set out in Table 5.2 (page 100).

Table 5.2 A self-assessment form for each professional standard

Professional standard

Phase 1: What do I already know?	What direct teaching have I had in relation to this standard?	For example: Qualifying training modules Seminars In-house courses Directed reading
	What other experiences have contributed to my knowledge about this standard?	For example: Work experiences Personal experiences Placements Reading, researching
Phase 2: What do I need to learn?	What gaps do I have in relation to this standard – what needs strengthening?	For example: Use of legislation, policy Multi-agency working Use of frameworks Agency procedures Specific skills
Phase 3: How am I going to learn it?	What work or other learning opportunities would meet the gaps I have identified?	For example: Types of cases Ways of working (observation, co-working, shadowing) Courses or training Resource packs or manuals Supervision Learning sets

Designing your professional development plan

The gaps identified in the self-assessment above define the areas for development which are carried into Stages 2 and 3 of the overall planning cycle, and become the objectives to be met in your development plan.

Box 5.6 Designing your professional development plan: checklist

Use the following questions in relation to each of your learning objectives to record your professional development plan in tabular form.

- What do I want to achieve?

- What sort of activity is involved?

- How soon do I need to do this (start date and expected completion)?

- What resources do I need (e.g. release; backfill; course costs)?

- Who can help me (e.g. human resources department; colleagues; other agency/professional; ASYE coordinator)?

- How will I know when I have achieved this objective?

- How and where will evidence be recorded and stored?

Finalising the first draft of your plan will necessitate some detailed discussions with your line manager and/or supervisor, and where relevant ASYE programme coordinator, to prioritise the learning you need to undertake and to agree how and when the range of activities identified will be made available to you. The aim is to design a coherent plan which explicitly links your evolving workload with your personal progress and the training opportunities planned for you. If it is to be a useful tool, your professional development plan needs to be used on a regular basis, by both you and your manager/supervisor. Stage 4 of the planning process is concerned with evaluating your progress, providing a direct link to monitoring changes and development in both supervision and the agency's formal appraisal processes. The outcomes from these discussions should then be recorded in a revised plan (Stage 5), bringing the full professional development planning cycle back to Stage 1 again, at which point you undertake a new self-assessment of your learning needs as the next step in your continuing professional development. Each cycle can be recorded and stored for future use in your professional development file (see Figure 1.1, page 34).

Key considerations for a successful induction

- Take the lead in ensuring that you discuss your record of achievement and future learning needs from your qualifying course in supervision.

- Formulate a written supervision agreement with your line manager, setting out your respective roles and responsibilities.

- Undertake a self-assessment of your learning needs in relation to the standards and capabilities relevant for your new post (including formal NQSW programmes), identifying any gaps and suggest a concrete plan to meet them.

- Use the objectives identified in the first cycle of your professional development planning process to make links to the training courses you plan to attend and the types of work you are undertaking.

Chapter 6

Roles and Tasks

- Definition of social work
- Initial expectations
- Personal motivations
- Initial confidence
- Core tasks
- Key considerations about roles and tasks

Having looked at induction, in this chapter we now explore some of the intended roles and tasks of social work and how these are linked to your motivations to join the social work profession in the first place. We take a look at your initial workplace confidence and turn to your initial expectations, exploring some of the early tensions between these and the demands of your organisation.

Definition of social work

On the face of it, a definition of social work would be a logical place to start thinking about roles and tasks. However, there is in fact no definition of social work on which all groups within the profession agree. Attempts to define what its proper activities should be, how its membership should be trained, what criteria should be applied to recruitment, and so on, become perennially entwined with long-standing debates about the centrality of particular theories, methods or principles, disputes about roles or functions, and disagreement about responsibility for an almost unending array of practical tasks – all of which play a part, but none of which suffices on its own to describe what is expected of the profession by employers or by qualified social workers themselves (Blewett, Lewis and Tunstill 2007). Each of the UK nations has undertaken a review of the roles, tasks and functions of social work in recent years (DHSSPS 2012 in Northern Ireland; GSCC 2008 in England; Asquith, Clark and Waterhouse 2005 in Scotland; and ADSS 2005 in Wales), from which a variety of 'typologies' have emerged, each of which has emphasised that 'tasks' cannot be considered without taking account of the interlocking nature of values and principles, as well as the contexts within which the various tasks of social work are carried out. These disparities underline the near impossibility of reaching one comprehensive, uncontested definition of social work. However, at the time of writing the *Roles and Functions of Social Workers in England: Advice Note*, produced in 2014 by The College of Social Work (TCSW 2014), is the most recent attempt to provide some specific guidance on the situations in which social workers *must* be involved and those where they *should* be involved as lead professionals, with examples of their roles and functions in these situations drawn from both adults' and children's services. These can make a helpful contribution to understanding the overall context in which social workers currently operate in England, and point to the contributions that social work can make to policy debates and development elsewhere. Updating its contribution to the debate, the International Federation of Social Workers has also proposed a new global definition of social work, which attempts to capture the profession's core mandates, principles, knowledge and practice in one place, as follows:

> Social work is a practice-based profession and an academic discipline that promotes social change and development, social cohesion, and the empowerment and liberation of people. Principles of social justice, human rights, collective responsibility and respect for diversities are central to social work. Underpinned by theories of social work, social sciences, humanities and indigenous knowledge, social work engages people and structures to address life challenges and enhance well-being. The above definition may be amplified at national and/or regional levels. (IFSW 2014)

Initial expectations

Newly qualified social workers are sometimes shocked by the limited amount of time that they get to undertake direct work with service users. Indeed, a major complaint from frontline social workers employed in all settings, but most particularly in local authorities, is that their work has become more bureaucratic and less client-focused in recent years (APPG/BASW 2013; Community Care 2005, 2006; Jones 2001; Statham, Cameron and Mooney 2006). Stalker and colleagues (2007) have identified that, even at times of considerable turbulence, 'work with clients' is the factor which contributes most to job satisfaction, and that the degree to which individual social workers feel that they have made a difference in people's lives is an important factor in sustaining their morale. It is not difficult to see the roots of these beliefs and satisfactions in the reasons which social workers give for making their choice of career, and it will be important to review your balance of time-use as you build up your workload and the focus of work in each case changes and develops.

A long-standing area of concern and frustration for many social workers is the weight of the paperwork with which they are required to deal. The reviews of social work undertaken in England (GSCC 2008), Scotland (Asquith *et al.* 2005), Wales (ADSS 2005) and Northern Ireland (DHSSPS 2012) all report on the pressures of bureaucracy caused by complex forms, problematic IT systems and performance management processes, with the consultation report by the Northern Ireland Social Care Council (Bogues 2008), for example, being entitled *People Work, Not Just Paperwork*. In our own research, among other things, the volume of paperwork frequently caused social workers at all career stages to work longer than their contracted hours on a regular basis, as exemplified by the following comment:

> Yes, at the moment, I'm probably only putting in about 4 or 5 hours overtime a week…the way social workers keep on top of their caseload is by working more than 37 hours a week. If you keep to the 37 hours you're paid for, you don't get done what needs to be done. (NQSW)

Despite the fact that one of the first recommendations from the Social Work Task Force (SWTF 2009b) was designed to reduce bureaucracy, it appears that little progress has been made to date with social workers continuing to find themselves 'chained to their desks by unwieldy IT systems' (APPG/BASW 2013, p.13). While the agreement on raising standards and tackling workload for teachers was specifically designed to reduce the excessive workload that entailed teachers spending two-thirds of their time on administrative tasks (DfES 2003), it is all the more lamentable that amidst a range of current reforms, such aims and outcomes have not been replicated, so far, for social workers.

Managing the bureaucratic burden

The *Standards for Employers of Social Workers in England and Supervision Framework*, developed by the Social Work Reform Board and now transferred to the Local Government Association, set out the expectation that all social workers should be provided with 'appropriate practical tools to do their job including effective case recording and other IT systems' (LGA 2014, p.10). It is envisaged that these expectations will be incorporated into the emerging self-regulation and improvement framework for public services to inform the revised inspection frameworks (LGA 2014), but at the time of writing the *Standards* provide only guidance and support for best practice development.

One of the problems associated with many current IT systems is that they are not flexible enough, for example restricting the amount of information that can be entered. Another common frustration in this area is the incompatibility between systems in different organisations, so that the transfer or sharing of information is not a straightforward process, often requiring 'double entry' of the same information on two or more systems.

> It's getting used to what the paperwork's like because I find it very constricting, having to sort everything into boxes. My boss is always saying 'make the boxes work for you' and that's very true. What I think she means by it is – understand what it's asking for and put in, in your own way. So having other colleagues around to talk to has helped. (NQSW)

So what can you do about the bureaucratic burden facing social workers? First of all, you should make sure that you get appropriate training on your employing organisation's IT system as soon as possible. You should also try to give yourself time just to experiment with it, to become familiar with its commands and navigate around it, as well as accessing some completed forms, reports and records of a more experienced member of staff to give you a better idea of how others are using the system, but 'making it work for you' is the priority here.

The IT skills that you used on your qualifying course should more than meet the standard required for most agency systems. Sometimes, the 'know how' is there in principle, but has to be delivered using unfamiliar processes within the constraints of limited time and resources, as recognised by this NQSW:

> I've learnt very quickly that you know what actually happens is a far cry from how we would ideally work with people and the restrictions in respect to resources and funding and what we can put in to support families. So I'm taking a deep breath and go, OK, if this what I've got to work with, what can I do with it? (NQSW)

You should also consider what use you are able to make of other resources. Are there administrative or clerical staff who can assist with data input, and are you able to delegate responsibility for some record keeping to others, while retaining oversight and case responsibility?

Personal motivations
Career choice

Clearly, your motivations for choosing social work as a career will have some bearing on your initial expectations and ultimate job satisfaction. Little research exists in this area, with one of the only studies to have explored the motivations of new recruits to social work having been undertaken over a quarter of a century ago (Pearson 1973). Nonetheless, the findings appear to be as valid today as they were in the 1970s, echoing those of our own research in which the reason most often quoted for choosing social work as a profession was 'wanting to help people – to make a difference', with little or no mention of personal career aspirations, higher status or improved income.

> I may not be able to effect a lot of change but for me, personally, I want to see that I actually try to make some sort of difference. (NQSW)

> It's the only reason I do this job really. I mean the money is part of it. Of course it is. It's a job. But I wouldn't be doing it for the money I get paid if I didn't actually want to try and make a difference to people's lives, because I do. And that's the thing that holds me to the job. (NQSW)

Pearson contended that those making the choice of social work as a career in the early 1970s were rejecting the aspirations typically associated with joining a profession, such as the acquisition of money, position and power, in favour of self-actualisation achieved through working for others. He further postulated that social workers' choice of career was an attempt to find a solution to the problems of society at large – in short, an attempt to 'inject dignity and authenticity into a life which threatens to be short on meanings' (Pearson 1973, p.217). How far do your own motivations match those of the social workers in the studies discussed here?

Achieving potential – hierarchy of needs

While you will almost certainly be familiar with Maslow's (1943) hierarchy of needs in relation to social work with service users, you may not have considered that the ascending stages towards achieving full potential might be equally relevant to your motivation to take up your career. Figure 6.1 sets this out, with your *basic needs* (met through a good induction) acting as the foundation on which the remainder of your professional development rests. In ascending order, this then involves establishing your *safety*, including arrangements for the supervision of your practice, and a sense of *belonging* to the team, organisation and profession of which you are now a member. Once these needs are met, you can then move on to building your personal *esteem*, involving the recognition of your achievements so far, and, finally, the *self-actualisation* posited by Pearson, when you are aspiring to reach your full potential as a confident and competent professional.

Figure 6.1 Achieving professional potential (adapted from Maslow 1943)

Initial confidence

Initial confidence in the workplace cannot be entirely separated from the way in which qualifying training is organised and delivered. The 'specialism versus generic' debate in relation to social work education and training has raged for many decades now (e.g. Seebohm 1968) and looks set to continue, particularly in the light of the development of fast-track training schemes for child care social workers, already discussed in the introduction to this book.

However training is undertaken, as we have noted earlier, the '*thud!*' that comes with the change in status from student to professional should not be underestimated. Socialisation into any new profession is a slow process in which the learning is qualitatively different from being a student, involving the application of skills and knowledge in practice situations where full case responsibility is held. Theories of adult learning (e.g. Schön 1983) help to make the links between learning and experience more explicit. In terms of your own professional development, it is clearly not enough simply to defer to the opinions of others – you must establish your own 'know how', which will mean reflecting critically upon your own developing experience, wrestling with the apparent anarchy of the workplace, and experimenting increasingly with your own ideas. Observation and discussion are useful developmental tools, but over time – and with support – your ultimate goal will be gaining the confidence to judge matters from your own perspective, finding what works best for you as an autonomous professional.

Professional competence

In accepting your name onto their respective registers, the care councils in the four UK countries are confirming that you are 'fully competent' to perform the role of social worker. However, we have already noted that whatever is learned during qualifying training represents only the beginning of professional learning, as noted by the following NQSW:

> I begin to realise that there is so much more that I don't know than I do. (NQSW)

A number of studies of professional development in health and social care (e.g. Eraut 1994; Yelloly and Henkel 1995) have suggested that the development of professional competence takes place on both a conscious and unconscious level. If competence can be conscious and unconscious, then it follows that incompetence is also likely to operate in these two domains, as represented in Figure 6.2 (Morrison 2001).

Conscious competence	Conscious incompetence
• What I know I know	• Openly acknowledged gaps
• What I know I can do	
• Clear transferable skills	
• Can be easily explained to others	
Unconscious competence	Unconscious incompetence
• What I know or can do without being conscious of how I know it	• Things which I am unaware I do not know
• Hard to explain to others	• Others may see gaps but I do not
• May be lost in times of turbulence or disruption and change	

Figure 6.2 A competence matrix (adapted from Morrison 2001)

The real danger area identified in the matrix is that of 'unconscious incompetence', as it is here that dangerous practice can take root. It is almost self-evident that, if professional learning develops 'by doing the job', then the quality and culture of your workplace will have a powerful influence over the ways in which your professional competence and capability is shaped. The greater your exposure to critically reflective evidence-based practice, clearly articulated values and cooperative working relationships, the more likely you will be to establish good habits, working styles and beliefs. By contrast, the habits developed in a stressed or dysfunctional working environment will tend to foster some elements of unconscious incompetence.

Core tasks

Social workers often refer to the variety of their work as a positive motivator, and the 14 core tasks identified in Box 6.1 (page 112) attest to the wide range of activities which might commonly be encompassed in a single day in the life of a social worker.

In any job there are, on the one hand, the parts that we enjoy quite naturally, and with which we can engage with real enthusiasm. On the other, there will always be elements which we find more challenging or less interesting, which will require more explicit effort and determination. Especially when you are under pressure, it is these irritating or worrisome elements that are likely to be uppermost in your mind. This is rather succinctly expressed by an anonymous aphorist who wrote that 'happiness writes white' (i.e. it is invisible), leaving you with the impression that everything at work is characterised by some degree of difficulty. To avoid developing a distorted impression of your day-to-day activities, it can therefore be helpful to gather some hard data of how you actually spend your own time at work, by completing the table in Box 6.1 over a period of, say, two weeks.

Box 6.1 Time spent on core tasks
WHAT TASKS TAKE UP YOUR TIME?

Keeping a record of core tasks over a period of, say, two weeks, will help you to see more broadly how you are spending your time.

		Working with parents/carers	Working with children	Working with groups and communities	Preparing reports For boards, panels, court	Evaluating and analysing Assessment information	Data entry; information management systems	Admin: correspondence/email	Liaising with other professionals	Liaising within team/agency	Supervision	Training/CPD activities	Allocation – meetings/discussion	Accessing research; internet and intranet	Travel
Week 1	Mon														
	Tues														
	Wed														
	Thurs														
	Fri														
Week 2	Mon														
	Tues														
	Wed														
	Thurs														
	Fri														

Key: Significant time ✓✓   Little time ✓   No time ✗

You can use this information to reflect on your own initial expectations about, for example, the amount of time you actually do spend doing direct work with service users, as well as to inform supervision discussions about your overall workload, type of work and future development opportunities.

Key considerations about roles and tasks

- Try focusing your expectations on a 'hierarchy of need', with good induction at the bottom of the triangle as the foundation on which you will be able to build your future development.

- Manage the burden of bureaucracy by ensuring you seek out IT training as soon as possible, and take time to familiarise yourself with the system and how to navigate it. It may be helpful to try to get access to the forms, reports and records of a more experienced member of staff to see how others are managing the various tasks.

- Consider what other resources could be available to you: are there administrative or clerical staff to assist you with data input, or could you delegate some record-keeping to others, remembering that you will need to retain oversight and case responsibility?

- Identify the range of core tasks relevant to your own particular post and review the balance of your time use between them. Some numerical data describing an average week could be really helpful in supervision to inform discussions designed to help you maintain a satisfying mix of tasks.

Additional Resources

Codes of practice

All four UK care councils require social workers and their employers to meet common standards set out in their individual codes of practice.

- For social workers, the codes describe expected standards of professional conduct and practice.
- For employers, the codes set out how employers should meet their responsibilities for managing and supporting their staff.

England

HEALTH AND CARE PROFESSIONS COUNCIL

Standards of proficiency – relevant to initial registration since March 2012: www.hpc-uk.org/publications/standards/index.asp?id=569.

Standards of conduct, performance and ethics – relevant to all social workers: www.hpc-uk.org/publications/standards/index.asp?id=38.

Local Government Association

Standards for Employers of Social Workers in England and Supervision Framework: www.local.gov.uk/documents/10180/6188796/The_standards_for_employers_of_social_workers.pdf/fb7cb809-650c-4ccd-8aa7-fecb07271c4a.

Northern Ireland – NISCC

Codes of Practice for social care workers and employers of social care workers: www.niscc.info/index.php/codes-of-practice.

Scotland – SSSC
Codes of practice for social service workers and employers.
www.sssc.uk.com/doc_details/1020-sssc-codes-of-practice-for-social-service-workers-and-employers.

Wales – CCW
Code of practice for social care workers: www.ccwales.org.uk/code-of-practice-for-workers.

Code of practice for employers of social care workers: www.ccwales.org.uk/code-of-practice-for-employers.

Continuing professional development (CPD)
PERSONAL DEVELOPMENT PLANNING
Chartered Institute of Personnel and Development. Generic guidance, advice, online tools and examples of personal development plans: www.cipd.co.uk/cpd/default.aspx.

SKILLS FOR CARE
Developing social workers' practice. Core principles for employers providing opportunities for social workers' continuing professional development: www.skillsforcare.org.uk/Social-work/Social-work-CPD/Continuing-to-develop-social-workers.aspx.

PART III

Jumping the Hurdles

- Chapter 7 Time management and the work/life balance
- Chapter 8 Finding support
- Chapter 9 Taking part in supervision

Part III focuses on the period after induction as you take on an increasing workload and begin to deal with some of the stresses as well as the pleasures of the job. We explore ways of finding support from a range of sources, including the team and a two-way 'supervisory alliance', as well as positive coping strategies for working in stressful situations.

Managing your tasks and time are the focus in Chapter 7 as your workload steadily increases, in size and complexity, over the next few months. The importance of managing the boundaries between work and home are emphasised to help you establish an appropriate work/life balance for your long-term health and well-being.

It is important to realise that all of the support you need cannot be found in one place, and Chapter 8 considers access to a range of different sources and types of support, to meet your needs in different situations and at different times, as an essential requirement for all social workers. Although it may feel imperative to prioritise tasks focused on service-user needs, it is equally important to take time to consider and prioritise your own needs.

Chapter 9 is devoted entirely to supervision – its participants and functions; its central place in providing support and guidance for all social workers; and the importance of your active participation in leading the agenda and preparing fully for each session. You need to remain mindful of the fact that even supervision – on its own – has its limits, and, if the work demands being placed on you are too great, the need to take positive action is unavoidable.

Chapter 7

Time Management and the Work/Life Balance

- Organisational demands
- Time management
- Establishing a healthy work/life balance
- Key considerations for better time management and a healthy work/life balance

In this chapter we consider some of the pressures which have led to the demands that social work organisations now place on their staff, and some of the tensions that exist between the agency's expectations and your own. We take a look at how well you are using your time to meet the organisational demands placed upon you, and identify some practical strategies which might help you to feel more in control of your workload. We consider the importance of establishing and maintaining a healthy work/life balance, against a background where many social workers feel that the normal working day is just not long enough to meet all the deadlines necessary.

Organisational demands

Social work organisations throughout the UK, and most particularly local authorities which are the main employers of social workers, are under almost constant pressure to improve their services, involving processes of change and reorganisation. The major drivers of change include:

- increasingly rigorous audit and inspection requirements, often resulting from the recommendations of inquiries into, for example, child abuse tragedies or failures to adequately safeguard vulnerable adults

- performance management targets and deadlines developed to meet the requirements of policy initiatives and legislative changes

- more complex funding streams and service delivery arrangements

- fewer resources accessed via ever-higher thresholds, leading to deeper, more entrenched presenting problems

- increasing public expectations of services, particularly in terms of limiting risk

- negative media representations of social work, and

- an increasingly litigious society, with service users and carers turning more readily to the courts.

Managerialism

Given this background, it is perhaps not surprising that social work organisations have tended to respond by embracing managerialist approaches to the delivery of their services. Marketisation and consumerism, driven by competitive tendering and almost constant efficiency improvement savings, can lead to the impression that budget management and the achievement of performance targets and deadlines, rather than best practice predicated on service-user need, is the agency's primary focus. All of this appears to be in direct opposition to the professional motivations and value base of many social workers, and there may be significant differences between the way in which you want to practise, and what the organisation you work for demands. These conflicting perspectives (Morrison 2001) are summarised in Table 7.1.

Table 7.1 Comparison of practitioner and organisational perspectives on work

Practitioner focus	Organisational approach
Process	Task
Relationship	Procedures
Outputs	Outcomes
Exploration	Rush for certainty
Mentoring	Monitoring
Depth	Surface
Change	Compliance
Context	Event
Continuity	Contract

In response to high profile inquiries into the ways in which failing services are delivered in both adult and children's services, there is an increasing need for agencies to protect themselves against liability and blame, and systems through which practices can be ordered, standardised, recorded and audited have been developed so that there is a clear audit trail from the bottom to the top of the organisation. The impression among frontline social workers, subjected to standardised practices and auditing, that their primary function is to keep the organisation safe, is often inescapable.

Under pressure to collect ever more information to meet the needs of regulation and external inspection, the requirement for data-gathering will inevitably mean an increase in the number, complexity and frequency of agency forms that have to be completed. Organisational systems of this sort tend to reduce any sense of personal obligation and responsibility, and processes which focus on ticking boxes can feel like an attempt to control your work, limiting your professional autonomy.

Where the meaning of your work is subsumed by a tide of bureaucracy, your motivation is likely to suffer. These losses can be accentuated at times by your emotional responses to the work. Depending on the particular situations in which you become involved at work, sadness, despair, anxiety or confusion may result, especially if you are not able to stand back and instead becoming enmeshed in the situation.

There will inevitably be times when you feel frustration and demoralisation at the lack of time or resources that are available for you to do your job. It will take time to come to your own resolution of the conflicts inherent in the system, between your professional ideals and the daily reality of work. As an NQSW it is unlikely that you will be able to influence these issues at a structural level, at least in the early stages of your career, but understanding what has driven a particular development may help you to appreciate some of the downward pressures within the organisation. It may simply be a salutary exercise to remember that the agency systems were developed in response to valid pressures, and that increasing experience will mean that you are able to streamline your approaches to the completion of all the documentation that is required of you.

Expectations of service users and carers

'Wanting to help people' is a primary motivation for most social workers, and keeping at the front of your mind the tasks which are valued most by those who use services should make an important contribution to helping you keep a balance between your own expectations and the demands of your agency.

Research reviewed by Statham *et al.* 2006 presents a clear picture of what is valued most by service users. This includes the importance of:

- developing and maintaining respectful and listening relationships, the nature of which is central to the way in which service users perceive the quality of the services they receive

- empowering relationships, treating people as individuals and demonstrating respect by recognising what is important to them, and that people are experts in their own lives

- personal qualities of honesty and reliability that inspire confidence, including not making promises that you cannot keep, and being honest about the resources available to deliver what service users want

- knowledge about local resources, which was highlighted in Chapter 1 as an important part of your early introduction and orientation in the agency

- continuity, which is primarily about being able to see the same person over time. This has organisational implications for the way in which work is allocated and specialisms are divided up, as well as the retention and support of staff to minimise sickness absence and turnover, and

- time to engage with service users, who believed that social workers needed more time to develop relationships.

More specifically, when children and young people were asked about the tasks carried out by social workers that they valued most (CSCI 2006), the following list emerged, with the most frequently cited issues at the top:

- help with personal problems

- being listened to

- help in staying safe

- getting ready to leave care

- someone to speak on their behalf

- information following a review

- getting the right placement to live in

- contacting family

- help to keep out of trouble

- getting access to personal file

- help to cope with bullying

- getting a passport.

In adult services, much social care policy and funding is now primarily directed towards person-centred support. Research carried out by the user-led Standards We Expect consortium and published by the

Joseph Rowntree Foundation (JRF 2011, p.3) has highlighted a range of key components valued by service users:

- putting the person at the centre, rather than fitting them into services

- treating service users as individuals

- ensuring choice and control for service users

- setting goals with them for support

- the importance of the relationship with practitioners

- listening to and acting on what service users say

- providing up to date, accessible information about appropriate local services

- being flexible, and

- taking a positive approach, highlighting what services users might be able to do, not what they cannot do.

Given the complex and often ambiguous nature of social work, in a context of almost endemic change, the challenge lies in recognising and working with all of the tensions and how they are managed within the organisation. Uncertainty and anxiety cannot be eliminated altogether, but the development of individual coping mechanisms and a range of sources of support (see Chapters 8–10), together with a satisfying organisational climate and workplace culture (see Chapter 11), are all needed if you are to maintain your morale and job satisfaction through your first year and beyond as a qualified social worker.

Time management
The demands of the organisations that employ social workers are many, and this means that your work is likely to be stressful at times, frequently involving interruptions and changing priorities. Skill is needed to organise and manage your time so that you can be confident that what needs to be done will get done at the appropriate time. 'A day in the life of a social worker' cannot be expressed in quite the

same tidy way that a teacher is able to use a timetable or a nurse a shift rosta, and this makes planning and managing time a more challenging task but one which will nevertheless produce dividends in helping you to develop a sense of control over your work.

Social work is a busy, pressurised job, and many social workers feel that the normal working day frequently does not provide enough time in which to meet all the necessary demands made of them. In the ebb and flow of your early professional life, working over your contract hours will be almost inevitable from time to time, and this is not in itself a bad thing. Perhaps working long hours reflects commitment, but it can also mean that you miss out on personal and leisure activities and time to relax and recover. You should remain alert to the danger of extending your working day on a regular basis, and seeing these additional hours as a mark of dedication, because in all probability your efforts are likely to be unappreciated. Making more effective use of your work time by prioritising tasks should mean that the times when work needs to spill over into your personal, family or leisure time are kept to a minimum.

Time-use survey

Managing time effectively requires you to take a realistic view about how much you can do and what you can reasonably expect of yourself, and then to plan ahead to meet the priorities. Completing the questionnaire in Box 7.1 (page 126) may help you to identify the areas where you can make some efficiency savings.

Managers have an important role to play in ensuring that the workplace is a time-efficient environment, and using the questionnaire above to look at time efficiency works even better if the whole team can be involved in scoring the statements, to develop an agenda for changing how everyone operates.

Box 7.1 Time use questionnaire
HOW EFFICIENTLY DO YOU USE YOUR TIME?

For each statement, choose the option which most closely reflects the way you work by putting a tick in one box in each row. The aim of the exercise is to mark everything as 'always'. If you have options marked in the other columns:

- Which of them could you move at least one column to the left?

- What do you need to change in order to make the move?

	Always	Usually	Sometimes	Rarely
I make and use a weekly plan				
I create blocks of time for big jobs				
I deal with interruptions effectively				
I deal with paperwork effectively				
I can find what I need easily on my desk				
I can find what I need easily in the recording system				
I can find what I need easily on the intranet				
Discussions with colleagues are to the point				
Team meetings are short and focused				
I delegate where possible and use others well				
My manager seems to respect my time				
I find time to relax outside work				
I plan my leisure activities and stick to them				
I feel in control of my working day				

Source: adapted from Thody, Gray and Bowden (2007)

Time management strategies

There are a number of guiding principles for good time management which should help you to make efficient use of your time at work. These include:

- planning ahead

- being clear about what you need to get done

- being aware of when potential problems, such as interruptions or your own habits, will make things difficult

- knowing when you can be flexible and when you can't

- having strategies for coping with problems when they occur

- not making extra work by being disorganised.

The checklist in Box 7.2 is designed to help you identify the 'pinch points' in your everyday work, where the workload mounts up and might threaten to overwhelm you.

Box 7.2 Time and tasks: checklist

Identify the routine things that you do every day.

- Do your feelings change with different tasks?

- Are there certain times of day when you are more tired or stressed?

- Do you allocate time to particular activities?

- How often do you spend just the allocated time on an activity? How often do you go over?

- What are your main time-wasters (e.g. interruptions, chatting, looking for something)?

- What avoidance routines do you indulge in?

Source: adapted from Siviter (2008)

PRIORITISING

Organising your workload means that you will need to set priorities, identifying those tasks that need to be done now and those that can safely be left until later. Using a filtering system to sort your work into daily, weekly and monthly deadlines is a good start in getting organised. For example, individual tasks can be grouped together into one of four categories:

1. Essential – to be done before anything else

2. Important – better done sooner rather than later

3. Routine – can wait until later

4. Of interest – for future reference.

Setting deadlines for important pieces of work is essential. Commit to a particular date, marked in your diary, which in good times will act as a reminder to keep you on track and in adversity will prompt you to review and reschedule your workload, according to new priorities and pressures.

TAKING CONTROL OF PAPERWORK AND EMAILS

To prevent the accumulation of a paper mountain on your desk, or a long list of emails on your computer, it is important to sort out this material on a routine basis. Do not give each piece of paper or electronic message equal weight or value. Instead, divide them into items which can simply be jettisoned, generally those that are of no direct relevance or use to you; those needing a quick or concise response that can be dealt with straightaway; and those that are important and need your detailed attention. As a general rule, try to handle each piece of paper or electronic message once only.

DELEGATING

It is almost certain that, at times, you will have too much to do. One person often cannot do everything, and delegating or sharing your work with others is an essential part of professional practice. Amidst all the competing pressures and demands on your time, it is important to be able to separate out the tasks that can only be done by you, and those that others might do safely and appropriately. You may think of delegation as one of the more challenging tasks for a new member of the team, but asking yourself some of the following questions when you are thinking about delegating a task to someone else could help to highlight any difficulties or pitfalls:

- What can only a qualified social worker do? What are the legal constraints and agency policy?

- Does the task require professional judgement or skilled social work intervention?

- Is there someone else with the necessary knowledge and skills to whom I might delegate this task, and, if so, what support will they need?

- If I do delegate a task, what would be the worst thing that could go wrong?

- Is there any reason I should not delegate the task; am I just being lazy?

- What is the best use of my time in the interests of service users and carers?

MANAGING INTERRUPTIONS

Interruptions can have a negative impact on your efficiency. If they come from service users there may be little that you can do about them. But interruptions can also come from inside and outside the office, from colleagues or other professionals. There are a number of ways of responding to these, but you must ensure that you do not become a victim of the pincer movement between a busy job and other people's demands. You must balance your needs with those of your colleagues, and learn not to feel guilty about prioritising your own needs.

HELP WITH SAYING NO

This may well be one of the most important skills in a busy, pressurised workplace. There is a real temptation when you are new to 'prove' your enthusiasm and commitment by accepting every task asked of you, or opportunity offered to you. However, ultimately this is not likely to be helpful, either to you or others. You can be professional and collegiate and still keep the demands on your time within reasonable limits. If you feel that you need help to say no, the following might prove useful strategies:

1. Delay the decision – request time to think about it.

2. Offer some support but opt out of taking on the full load.

3. Say that you would like to help but that you have to work on other priority tasks at the moment.

4. Propose an alternative arrangement that is more manageable for you.

Establishing a healthy work/life balance

Newly qualified social workers can struggle at times to manage the duality of their role: balancing personal involvement in people's lives with the ability to stand back, make judgements and reach often hard decisions. You may find that it is difficult to leave your concerns for service users behind at the end of the working day, allowing feelings of anxiety to percolate from work into your personal life, giving rise to increased levels of stress. This can be amplified for those who live alone, whose partners are working abroad, or who have caring responsibilities for relatives. The extra burden of stress brought into the workplace by those in caring professions who are inadequately supported in their caring responsibilities at home has been reported by Wharton and Erickson (1995), as well as in our own research with NQSWs. There is also some evidence that balancing these different sources of stress has a particularly negative effect on job satisfaction for women. As the vast majority of social workers are women, these findings might be considered particularly pertinent.

Feelings of stress and anxiety are common among all those joining a new profession, and understanding, help and support will be needed to enable you to establish an appropriate work/life balance if you are not to feel overwhelmed. The 'rebalancing' mechanisms have been more fully reported in relation to other professions, such as nursing (Gerrish 2005; Maben and Macleod Clark 1998; Mooney 2007) and teaching (Parkinson and Pritchard 2005), but rather different pressures and working practices seem to apply to the newly qualified staff in these occupations compared to social work. For example, nurses do not bear case responsibility for individual patients in quite the same way as social workers, and, to some extent, the wearing and removing of a uniform, coupled with the handover to another team at the end of each shift, defray some of the burden in a way not usually available to social workers. And, for teachers, since the introduction of a formal probationary year in 1999, a workload reduction has been obligatory for the first 12 months in post, and all qualified teachers are provided with time away from the classroom (non-contact time) for planning and assessment. As we have already noted, teachers are also not expected to carry out a range of specified clerical duties, such as data input.

The formal programmes for NQSWs, such as ASYE and AYE, should help reduce some of the demands and increase the support available to them in their first year of employment, but, as noted in Chapter 1, the present arrangements are not mandatory in England, or universally available across the UK, and even if you are registered on one of these programmes, it will still be helpful for you to monitor your time and tasks for discussion in supervision.

Achieving an appropriate balance

Growing evidence shows that people who work extended hours actually end up producing less, rather than more. Achieving a healthy work/life balance means different things to different people, but it is important to achieve a balance which means that you are working to have a satisfying and healthy life, rather than simply living to work. Proper sleep, a balanced diet and physical exercise all have a part to play in minimising the negative effects of a stressful job. Maintain a healthy separation between work and home by confining your work to the office, and practise working only within your designated hours, trying to eliminate or at least minimise the occasions on which you take work home. This is a very important boundary which should not be breached lightly. However, the increasing trend, particularly in local authorities, towards large, open plan office accommodation and hot desking arrangements, can militate against this important separation, especially where the lack of a quiet space for report writing or a confidential telephone call, for example, makes some home working almost unavoidable.

Preserving breaks and leave

As a general rule, you should take your daily lunch break. The way you spend your break can also serve either to energise you or to sap your strength. Getting outside for a short walk can improve your sense of well-being, and chatting with positive people, not malcontents, can nourish a good mood.

It is also important to make sure that you preserve your annual leave, other days off and any study days to which you are entitled. Try to use the time available to you at weekends and during holidays to focus on yourself and your family and friends. Well-planned relaxation and time to pursue your own interests will mean that you can return to work refreshed.

Key considerations for better time management and a healthy work/life balance

- Effective time management is primarily about getting organised, setting priorities and having a system which will allow you to track progress and review deadlines.

- Plan ahead – setting daily, weekly and monthly deadlines can be helpful.

- Be clear about priorities – group your tasks into one of four categories: essential/important/routine/of interest.

- Working over your contract hours will be almost inevitable from time to time and this is not, in itself, a bad thing, but be aware of the danger of extending your working day on a regular basis; the additional hours are unlikely to be appreciated in the way you might like or expect.

- Try to resist the very real and understandable temptation when you are new to prove your enthusiasm and commitment by accepting every task asked of, or opportunity offered, to you – learn how to say no.

Chapter 8

Finding Support

- Mapping your support networks
- Personal resources
- Support from others
- Organisational support
- Key considerations in finding support

This chapter aims to identify the specific support needs of NQSWs, exploring the structure of teams and their place in providing personal and professional support, together with the role of wider social support networks, both inside and outside the organisation.

Support has three main functions, each linked to a range of coping mechanisms (see Chapter 10). At a very basic level, support can take the form of practical advice and information, as part of problem-focused coping, which involves gathering information and identifying practical options. Support can also be a part of emotion-focused coping, when there is a need for help with your feelings in facing a difficult situation or dealing with its aftermath. The third function is to support healthy emotional adjustment, facilitated by talking, which can help you to cope with stress. Disclosure of stressful events and talking about the emotions associated with them is more likely to lead to positive readjustment when there are supportive networks (Lepore, Ragan and Jones 2000).

Studies looking specifically at social work have shown the importance of NQSWs having a *range* of different sources of support available to them, at different times, as they move through induction, transition and beyond (Collins 2008; Guerin, Devitt and

Redmond 2010; Stalker *et al.* 2007; Takeda *et al.* 2005). An early theme to emerge from our own research (see Table 8.1 on page 139) is the central importance of the people who are part of your team, networks and management structures in helping you to settle in and develop confident and competent practice during your first twelve months or so in post. You should therefore ensure that you make the best of every opportunity to build networks of relationships, both inside and outside your organisation. Support in all its guises – from your own personal resources; from others, at home and at work; both formal and informal – will help you to balance the oscillating levels of stress which are an almost inevitable part of the job. The relationship is represented diagrammatically in Figure 8.1.

Support and well-being

Stress and exhaustion

Figure 8.1 Relationship between workplace stress and support

Mapping your support networks

You may already be familiar with eco-mapping as a tool used by social workers to make an assessment of a service user's social relationships, but it is an approach equally applicable to your own social support networks. It can provide a dynamic overview of your circumstances, highlighting important connections and sources of support (as well as deficits and barriers) essential for your well-being, both now and in the future. According to Warren (1993), an eco-map is:

> An ecological metaphor [that] can lead social workers to see the client not as an isolated entity for study, but as a part of a complex ecological system. Such a view helps them to focus on the sources of nurturance, stimulation and support that must be available in the intimate and extended environment to make possible growth and survival. (Warren 1993, p.40)

To complete your own eco-map, you first need to identify the people or resources that are significant in supporting your learning and development, and some examples are suggested in Box 8.1 (page

136). Personalise this by filling in the blank circles and removing or adding new ones, as necessary. Draw lines to each circle to make the connections that exist in your network, describing those relationships by:

Using different lines to indicate the nature of the relationship, for example:
━━━ Practical; ——— Emotional; – – – Information/Advice;
• • • • • Critical

Adding a number (or a different colour) for the quality of the support, for example:
1 = strong; 2 = tenuous; 3 = distant; 4 = stressful;
5 = non-existent

Putting arrows on each line to signify the direction of help (or stress) for example:
flow both ways ←→ ; flow to you ← ; flow from you →

Adding a symbol for how frequently you call on that support, for example:
● Daily; ☐ Weekly; ■ Monthly; ◆ Few times per year

However creatively you are able to complete the exercise, the real strength of any eco-map lies in its simple, visual impact. It collects and organises not only a great deal of factual information but also displays, all on one side of A4 paper, the relationships between the important variables so that connections, themes and qualities are all brought into sharp focus for you.

Once you have it completed, use your eco-map to help you consider some of the following questions:

- Am I getting the sort of support I need?

- What is missing? What can I do to bridge any gaps?

- Which sources of support do I find most helpful/unhelpful?

- What actions can I take to foster and maintain them/reduce their impact?

- Which areas need strengthening? What action can I take to build up my network?

Box 8.1 Eco-mapping your workplace support system

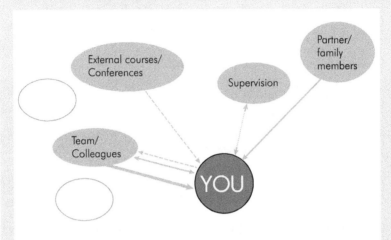

Significant Supports
Other possible sources to add as circles in the eco-map:
- In-house training/workshops
- Case study discussions
- Shadowing / co-working
- Special interest/practice groups
- Learning sets
- Friends
- Meetings
- Other professionals
- Study days
- Professional association/union
- Online forums/blogs/discussion groups
- Course tutor
- Ex-student/peer group

Personal resources
Job crafting

As we have already noted in Chapter 6, finding meaning in doing a worthwhile job plays a central role for many in making the choice of social work as a career, and finding significance and a sense of purpose in your work can also help you to deal with its inevitable stresses. There is evidence that even in the most restricted jobs employees can exert some influence over job boundaries and tasks to achieve a more positive sense of meaning and self-worth in their work. This has been called 'job crafting' (Wrzesniewski and Dutton 2001), which recognises the importance of personal control over even seemingly small matters. By taking control of or reframing some of the tasks, conditions or purposes of the work, 'job crafters' are able to make the job their own, creating new possibilities for self-accomplishment and mastery. Job identities are never fully determined by formal job descriptions, and resourceful job crafters will seek out the areas of latitude to actively reshape the tasks and social relationships of their role in a way that enables a more positive sense of self to be expressed and confirmed by others. Fostering this kind of mindset might relieve, for instance, some of the weight of bureaucracy which so often threatens to eclipse much of the day-to-day satisfaction in the social work role.

Making use of positive emotions

Positive emotions can also help to reduce levels of stress by 'quieting or undoing' negative emotions. Primary appraisal of a stressful situation offers you the opportunity to interpret it as one in which there is the possibility for change and gain, stimulating positive emotions such as eagerness, confidence, happiness and pride. States of stress can be differentiated along a continuum as shown in Figure 8.2.

Distress/ chaos	⟷	Anxiety/ stress	⟷	Eagerness/ excitement	⟷	Happiness/ pride

Figure 8.2 The stress continuum

Positive emotions are just as much a part of managing stress as negative ones, and they are the active ingredients in learning to cope with life's setbacks, transforming what starts out as emotional chaos into containable anxiety, so that with each experience, you acquire skills that will enable you to cope more effectively in the future. Over time, ongoing positive emotions build a lasting personal resource which can be utilised to encourage you to think with more flexibility, openness and creativity, which are important components of good professional practice.

Taking a proactive approach

As discussed in Chapter 7, there are also a number of proactive ways in which you can manage competing demands in the workplace. These include establishing a healthy work/life balance, managing your time effectively, taking breaks from your work, confining your work to your normal hours and place of work wherever possible, and learning to say no. It can also be helpful to recognise your peak energy times, so that you can arrange to do the most demanding tasks when your energy level is at its highest, reserving more routine work for the low points of your daily energy cycle.

Box 8.2 Seeking and finding support

Reflect on your own experiences in your current post:

- What sources of support are available to you?

- Can you identify three resources – people or activities – that you find particularly helpful?

- Can you identify three resources – people or activities – that you find unhelpful?

- Can you identify any gaps?

- What would you add, if anything?

Support from others

How would you describe your own experiences of seeking and finding different sources of support from others? What kinds of support are most important to you?

Responses to similar questions among NQSWs in our research are summarised in Table 8.1.

Table 8.1 NQSWs' sources of support

Source of support	Important /very important (%)
Formal, planned supervision	92
Colleagues in same team	92
Other professionals	92
Colleagues elsewhere in same agency	77
Friends and/or family	77
Peer/student from qualifying programme	38
Tutor/teacher from qualifying programme	8

We discuss the central role of supervision for the quality of your practice and professional development in Chapters 5 and 9, so here we will focus on the support provided by colleagues, wider professional networks and friends and family members.

Colleagues

In the early stages of your career, you may well be feeling anxious and in need of reassurance about your practice, and it is clear from the table above that the support of an experienced member of staff in the same team or elsewhere in the organisation can be a valuable resource, not only for emotional support, but also to provide you with opportunities to work alongside them, observing, shadowing or co-working, to build your knowledge and confidence. As discussed in Chapter 4, some organisations have adopted the practice of identifying a particular person to act as a mentor or buddy to support a new member of staff through the first few weeks in post, by offering help, information and advice. The role of a buddy is generally short-term, and is likely to be most effective and helpful when taken up by a willing volunteer, sited close to you (e.g. in the same team/ room), but offices where hot desking is the rule are likely to make this arrangement more difficult to implement and much less effective.

Mentoring may be a longer term arrangement, held in place for, say, the first 12 months in post. At its best, mentoring should involve a more experienced practitioner guiding and supporting a new member of staff through the initial transition period, smoothing the way by building confidence, knowledge and skills. There are many models of mentoring, and arrangements can vary from an informal personal link to much more formal, contracted arrangements. There may be some crossover with a supervisor or line manager, and, if you do have a named mentor, it will be important to be clear about respective roles, responsibilities and boundaries. Ideally, a mentor should be outside your line management arrangements, and there are benefits which parallel what other professions, such as medicine and nursing, would call clinical supervision, including opportunities to:

- discuss your work in confidence with someone who listens and understands the pressures of the job

- get feedback and new ideas about how to deal with work situations

- receive help in dealing with emotions engendered by the work, including stress and exhaustion, as well as excitement and happiness

- develop your knowledge of the organisation and how best to use its structures, processes and procedures, and

- enhance your sense of belonging and value as part of the team.

Wider professional networks

As noted in the introduction to this chapter, there are a number of straightforward or more instrumental reasons for seeking support from a wider network of colleagues, 'specialists' and other professionals. The need, particularly in the early days of a new post (at whatever point in your career), for practical advice, information and assistance will be obvious. As we noted in Chapter 4, time to put together your own list of key players, with particular areas of interest or expertise, both inside and outside your own organisation and professional boundaries, should be a key part of the initial orientation into your new surroundings.

Team meetings can also be used to good advantage if time is allowed for sharing common experiences, acknowledging strengths, and providing opportunities to explore problems and possible solutions, rather than simply focusing on bureaucratic allocation and procedural matters. This helps to prevent feelings of isolation, in which difficult decisions have to be made alone, without a collective forum in which to discuss them, either before or after the event, as illustrated by the following comment from a final-year social work student:

> And I think one of the reasons that I'm thinking of working in a hospital-based team is because I've just really enjoyed having the support of all these other disciplines around me to help make decisions. (Final-year social work student)

You might also take the initiative to look for wider support networks through professional associations, websites and associated electronic forums specific to your specialism, setting or interest, to establish 'communities of practice', particularly if geographical location is an additional isolating factor. This could be a useful approach to keeping in touch, for instance, with your peer group from qualification, or establishing a network of contacts following a successful training course.

Friends and family members

Table 8.1 on page 139 shows that more than three-quarters of the NQSWs who participated in our research placed great importance on the support they received from friends and family members. This informal support, beyond the workplace, is more valuable, perhaps, because it is free from the structural and power differentials which are an intrinsic part of organisational life. Friends and family act as a primary resource when moral support, reassurance and understanding are needed, as part of the emotion-focused coping which assists a return to positive, problem-solving strategies, as illustrated in the following quotation:

> And although you say that you don't bring work home, but you do and to have someone at home who understand and who's not going to judge you or think that you're doing something for the wrong reasons is the best support. (NQSW)

Talking has long been the cornerstone of many psychotherapeutic interventions, helping to vent and resolve the thoughts and feelings immediately provoked by stressful situations (Lepore *et al.* 2000), thereby facilitating adjustment to the stressor, and William Wordsworth expressed something of the enduring importance of talking when he wrote:

> A timely utterance gave that thought relief, and I again am strong. (Ode: *Intimations of Immortality from Recollections of Early Childhood*, 1807)

There are some interesting differences in relation to gender and support (Collins 2008). For instance, it has been shown that the more support a woman receives from her partner, the less conflict she experiences between job and family demands (Berkowitz and Perkins 1984). Women are generally better than men at looking for and providing social support for each other, and also tend to derive more satisfaction from it (Taylor *et al.* 2000). However, although typically neither so ready to look for nor to provide social support, it has been noted that men frequently receive support from a close female friend or partner (Kirschbaum *et al.* 1995). Taylor and colleagues (2000) have attempted to explain these gender differences as an adaptation by women of the general fight or flight response to threats, transforming this into behaviours which focus on nurturing (tending) and gathering into social groups (befriending) in order to reduce risk, threats or stress.

Organisational support
The team
In local authority and joint agency settings, the team is the most often cited repository of safety and nurture for NQSWs, as demonstrated in Table 8.1 (see page 139) and the following quotations from the same study:

> Yeah, brilliant, yeah, I will say the one thing that seems to hold social services together is the team, the camaraderie, the support that everybody gets, you do feel part of something. (NQSW)

Yes, I am... I'm well-supported and although the rest of the team aren't social work qualified, they're great. (NQSW – Joint Agency Team)

However, social work teams are no longer as homogeneous as they once were, and the need for coordination between, for example, education and children's services, or health and social care services, has resulted in the development of more multidisciplinary teams. The deployment of different professionals within multidisciplinary teams brings with it a range of advantages, as well as specific challenges. On the positive side, practitioners working within multidisciplinary teams report high levels of job satisfaction, linked to perceptions of a more creative and holistic approach to delivering services and a 'sense of liberation' from the narrow constraints of individual agency cultures (DCSF 2008). However, there are also a number of challenges which have implications for the availability of support. These include potential conflicts over roles and responsibilities amidst a range of professional backgrounds and cultures, as well as practitioners undertaking similar tasks but on rather different terms and conditions, as a result of historical agreements applicable to each individual's 'home' agency or profession.

Table 8.2 Stages in the formation of a team

Stage	Team behaviour
Forming	Purpose and goals may be unclear Stage marked by formality and politeness
Storming	Tensions emerge; team members struggle for position Leaders have to establish their authority
Norming	Team gains confidence and begins to feel a sense of identity; there is a growing consensus on approaches, goals, communication and leadership; members take on more responsibilities
Performing	Team becomes self-organising; members take full responsibility for tasks and relationships and work proactively for the benefit of the group; team achieves effective and satisfying results and recognises its achievements; levels of trust and confidence are high.

Source: adapted from Tuckman (1965)

Whatever the composition of the team you are joining as an NQSW, to help you understand something of the functioning of the group it is worth considering its stage of development, for example in terms of Tuckman's (1965) model, summarised in Table 8.2 (page 143).

It is worth bearing in mind that the stages of team formation are not static, and an individual team will move up and down through these different stages at different times as its membership and circumstances change (see Box 8.3).

Box 8.3 Storming or performing?

Apply Tuckman's stages to the groups or teams of which you are a part.

- What stage is each group or team currently at?

- What are the implications for your own support?

- How can you influence the way the groups or teams operate?

Teams can offer you positive support by providing:

- a source of meaning and identity

- learning opportunities which draw on the interests and expertise of others

- social interactions ranging from satisfactory working relationships through to close friendships

- motivation to keep you going in stressful situations, and

- shared responsibilities, helping you to build emotional strength and confidence.

On the other hand, teams can have their limitations where:

- team members are negative and unsupportive

- power is abused, and decision-making appears driven by politics rather than the needs of service users or team members, and

- competition between members, for funds or jobs for example, becomes destructive and damaging.

Whatever type of team you are working in when you start your career, there are some basic characteristics that you will certainly want to know about, which may influence the support that they are likely to offer to a new member. For instance:

- *Stability and state of the team:* If there are several fairly new members of the team, they are likely to remember very well what it was like to be new and welcome you readily. If the team is composed of mainly well-established staff, unaccustomed to change, then it may be more difficult to join in, particularly if there is something of a 'club' culture. This type of team may have become set in its ways, and may feel threatened by the changes heralded by a new member. In these circumstances, you may need to tread more carefully.

- *Leadership style:* How hierarchical is the organisational structure? To what extent does the team operate democratically? Are decisions made by consultation or sent down 'from above'?

- *Communication:* How does the team communicate? How often does the whole team come together? What opportunities are there for formal and informal communication?

- *Relationship among members:* Is your team a close-knit community or a loose association of members? How much real collaboration and cooperation is there? What sorts of relationships predominate? See Belbin (2004) for descriptors of different individual roles within teams.

Your answers to some of these questions will help you to form at least an initial understanding of the team's strengths and the way in which it operates. Having gathered this background information you could give some thought to any gaps, and what your own particular contribution to the team could be.

Group support and learning sets

It has been shown that, generally speaking, support from colleagues is far more efficacious in buffering the negative effects of workplace stressors than the provision of training in coping skills (Collins 2008). In this context, the support provided by groups and learning sets has much to recommend it, and, linked to the coping strategies discussed in Chapter 10, should help you by:

- encouraging discussion, providing opportunities for 'letting off steam' as an initial coping mechanism in stressful situations

- building consensus and providing you with opportunities to form coalitions and networks which will be important as part of a positive reappraisal approach to coping

- enhancing your own sense of role and mission, to prevent depersonalisation and promote self-detachment to protect against emotional exhaustion, and

- providing a forum for the wider exploration of the agency's implicit and explicit rules, role ambiguities and possible conflicts, all of which are primary causes of stress (see Chapter 10).

It became clear quite early on in our own research that NQSWs, like the one quoted below, needed a safe place in which to discuss their work and find release for their emotional responses to it, which varied from exhaustion and frustration, right through to anger, at times.

> I think there is a level of care and concern but whether it extends beyond 9–5 Monday to Friday I'm not sure. I'm seeing it in front of my eyes. People I thought were very strong are just breaking down in tears…and I think is anyone actually listening to what's going on? And they're not because they [management] are just driving, this machine just keeps driving and pushing and there's no let up with it… We're just this sort of cannon fodder if you want, just feeding this machine… And that's driving my life…being forced on my life and I'm thinking bloody hell… We need a revolution to go on here! (NQSW)

In fact, faced with the high levels of stress and anxiety commonly felt in frontline social work practice, it is especially important that you feel that you have 'permission' to express angry feelings appropriately. There is even some evidence to suggest that there is a negative effect on outcomes for service users if anger remains cooped up inside individual workers (Bednar 2003). We also make reference in Chapter 10 to the negative effects on individual coping where difficulties are internalised and allowed to build up in the hope that they will disappear. The difficulty for individuals frequently lies in finding a safe forum in which to express emotions safely. Supervision or team meetings may very well not provide the right environment for such self-disclosure, especially when you are a new member. In some agencies, groups of workers in a similar situation are facilitated to come together on a regular basis, in addition to their normal supervision, for the purposes of mutual support. NQSWs are a particularly good example of a readily identifiable group with specific support and development requirements, as the following quote illustrates.

> That's been really good, you know. A few of us get together and talk about where we are and how practice relates to university, or how it doesn't quite often. (NQSW)

A peer support group or learning set can provide the time and opportunity needed to consider yourself and your own needs in an appropriate environment, and certainly in England, these are an important element of the additional support included for NQSWs in ASYE programmes, reflected in the following comment:

> Yeah, like a local training centre would be booked and what worked really well with the monthly sessions, with all the NQSWs in the area, then what was really good was that I could then start networking with other NQSWs in different teams which was really helpful. (NQSW participating in an ASYE programme)

Ideally, such meetings should be held away from individual workplaces, and preferably be facilitated by someone outside of the agency's line management structures. Arrangements should also be fixed in advance, with meetings taking place at regular intervals, so that you can block out the time in your diary and firmly commit to being part of the group. There is a responsibility on the part of each member to attend regularly and to make an active contribution to the group for mutual benefit. Meetings like this provide members with a safe space in which to express their feelings, giving access to the social support of others in a similar position, as well as offering a forum for the exchange of information and advice. Join, if your agency already has these groups in place and where the message has not yet taken root, seize the initiative and suggest some of the benefits to your training or staff development department.

Training and development activities

Nearly all NQSWs are enthusiastic about taking on new tasks, developing new areas of their practice and continuing to learn. One way in which organisations can create a satisfying climate for social workers is by offering frequent opportunities for them to attend conferences, seminars, workshops and training programmes, and local authorities and larger voluntary sector organisations will definitely have a range of courses on offer. Much of the early in-house training offered to you as an NQSW is likely to be practical information or task-based, focusing on induction requirements and preparation for taking on more complex work. However, as well as focusing on enhancing the skills needed to undertake work with service users, you might also try to seek out and prioritise some sessions covering the following areas, to support your own development, recognising the additional stresses of transitional change from qualification into the workplace:

- stress management and resilience

- coping skills

- managing positive emotions

- time management

- managing change.

As the following quotations illustrate, it is not unusual for there to be little structuring of in-house training and continuing professional development opportunities, so you may need a good deal of determination, initiative and individual motivation to seek out what is available and how to book yourself a place.

> I'm not sure really. I don't think they have an actual policy about how it works. It's just that some people seem to do post-qualifying training and others...never do it. (NQSW)

Overall, there's a good level of training offered...but it's a bit hit and miss who gets on it and who doesn't...and it's, well you pick up the phone and find out what's on and you go and hassle your manager to give you a signature. (NQSW)

Organisations employing NQSWs have a responsibility to provide you with professional development opportunities, but it is your responsibility to ensure that you make the best use of what is available to you, in order to:

- meet your changing needs as you progress through induction, transition and any formal NQSW programme on which you are registered

- expand your areas of special interest, considering how these 'fit' with the organisation's overall aims and vision, and

- explore opportunities to broaden your experiences in a range of settings and contexts.

It is also important to remember to record what you have done for post-registration training and learning purposes and to update your professional development plan, so that the learning from each activity is brought together to provide a holistic picture of your ongoing development.

Key considerations in finding support

- The support you are likely to need as an NQSW cannot be found in one place. Access to a range of different sources and types of support, to meet your needs in different situations and at different times, is an essential requirement for all social workers, and time spent in developing a robust system for yourself is a sound investment for your future well-being.

- Although it may feel imperative to prioritise tasks focused on service user needs, there is an equal imperative to take time to find a safe place in which you can explore the impact of the work on yourself, and in which you have permission to express your feelings. If there are specific groups for newly qualified social workers, particularly as part of formal NQSW programmes such as ASYE in England, you should make regular attendance a personal commitment.

• The team is an important source of support, but it is not a static entity, and its character will change and evolve over time as well as in response to new pressures and personalities.

Chapter 9

Taking Part in Supervision

- The purpose and functions of supervision
- The dynamic structure of supervision
- Making the most of supervision
- Managing the tensions of supervision
- Key considerations for making the most of supervision

Supervision is widely recognised as a key learning and support mechanism, not only in the early stages but throughout the whole of your professional career in social work (SCIE 2012). The review of social work carried out by the SWTF (Baginsky *et al.* 2010) recognised the importance of the informal and peer supports discussed in the previous chapter, but also stressed the central role of one-to-one supervision. This chapter is therefore dedicated entirely to that subject, and is called 'taking part in supervision' to emphasise the collaborative nature of the process, and the need for each participant to take responsibility for their part in establishing a supportive 'supervisory alliance'.

Drawing on the recommendations of the SWRB (2010), some useful guidance about the frequency and duration of individual supervision sessions is beginning to emerge. For example, in England, supervision sessions are expected to last at least an hour and a half of uninterrupted time and should take place weekly for the first six weeks of employment for an NQSW, fortnightly for the next six months, and at least monthly thereafter. In addition, there is an expectation that social workers should have access to professional supervision provided by a registered social worker. However, the existence of a formal policy or protocol will not necessarily guarantee the delivery of appropriate supervision and support. As integrated working in multidisciplinary teams is becoming increasingly common, for example in hospital discharge or mental health services, you may find yourself in a situation where line management is separated from some of the more reflective and professional development aspects of supervision, provided by a senior practitioner or someone external to your own organisation, and we take a closer look at these 'shared' arrangements a little later in this chapter.

While formal NQSW programmes – ASYE in England and AYE in Northern Ireland – are likely to ensure that the frequency and duration of supervision outlined above are adhered to in the workplace, the care councils in Scotland and Wales have eschewed this 'one size fits all' approach, preferring that arrangements for supervision be the subject of individual contractual agreements. However, they too have recently provided guidance documents – *Practice Governance Framework* (Scottish Government 2011) and *Making the Most of the First Year in Practice* (CCW 2008) – setting out in broad terms what should be included in a good supervision contract. Going a little further, the *Standards for Employers of Social Workers in England and Supervision Framework*, developed by the Social Work Reform Board and now hosted by the Local Government Association (LGA 2013), set out what social workers in England should expect from their employers, including 'four key elements' of effective social work supervision, namely:

- the quality of decision-making and interventions

- line management and organisational accountability

- caseload and workload management, and

- the identification of further personal learning, career and development opportunities.

However, despite these frameworks and further guidance, as well as training and support for managers responsible for providing them (e.g. CWDC 2009), experiences of social work supervision and reports of its quality remain very variable (Baginsky *et al.* 2010; Carpenter *et al.* 2012). The following comments from our research with NQSWs are typical of those made by many social workers, newly qualified or not, when asked about their experiences of supervision:

> What we do is we review the cases very quickly...to see, as much as anything else, if there's any more space to fit some more cases in and it's a question of 'have you done this on time, have you done that on time' because my manager is under pressure [from senior managers].

> I'd like more time, more direction in terms of you know being able to sit down and get guidance when I'm approaching tasks.

> If the managers aren't given more time or there are no more managers, then what gives? Well it's the time particularly to reflect on cases...what did you do...what worked...what didn't...what have you learned... That's missing from all of our supervision. (Social workers – 12 months post-qualification)

As these comments reflect considerable dissatisfaction with at least some aspects of supervisory arrangements, it might be helpful to review your own experiences to date, using the exercise in Box 9.1.

Box 9.1 Supervision style
Thinking your experiences of supervision, either in your present job or from your qualifying training, what did you learn about:

- What supervision means for you?
- How you want to use supervision?
- What worries you most about supervision?
- What sort of supervision seems to suit you best?

The exercise may have pointed out a number of tensions inherent in the supervisory relationship, which may be particularly acutely felt when you are new to the organisation. So what should supervision do?

The purpose and functions of supervision

The overall purpose of supervision is to improve the services that are offered to service users and carers. Benefits for service users and carers may accrue directly, as supervision helps you to think about the best ways of helping them, on an individual basis, as well as indirectly, as better services are known to be delivered by satisfied social workers who feel that they are valued members of a committed team.

According to Kadushin (1976), supportive supervision should allay anxiety, reduce guilt, increase certainty and conviction, relieve dissatisfaction, fortify flagging faith, affirm and reinforce the worker's assets, replenish depleted self-esteem, nourish and enhance the capacity for adaptation, alleviate psychological pain, restore emotional equilibrium, comfort, bolster and refresh. Such an extensive list makes it clear why supervision is one of the most important mechanisms available to organisations for supporting and developing their staff.

Definitions of supervision in social work have been evolving for over half a century (Kadushin 1976; Morrison and Wonnacott 2010; Robinson 1936; Shulman 1982) and the supervisor–worker relationship has been described as the key encounter between the influence of organisational authority and professional identity (Middleman and Rhodes 1980). The '4x4x4 integrated model of supervision' used in materials to support supervisors working with early NQSW programmes delivered in children's services in England between 2009 and 2011 introduced 'mediation' as a fourth function of supervision to emphasise the dynamic nature of the supervision process and to situate it clearly within the wider organisational context (Morrison and Wonnacott 2010). However, although there are some significant differences between the various definitions of supervision, broad agreement has remained about the three main functions, which are:

1. *Normative* (sometimes called organisational or managerial)

   ○ implementing and monitoring policies, procedures, planning and budgeting

   ○ monitoring and auditing casework

   ○ ensuring competent, accountable practice.

2. *Restorative* (sometimes called personal or supportive)

   ○ providing emotional support and team building

   ○ promoting communication, coordination and cooperation.

3. *Formative* (sometimes called educational or developmental)

   ○ developing professional skills, techniques and boundaries

   ○ developing knowledge, drawing on detailed discussions of individual work.

The dynamic structure of supervision

It was Mattinson (1981) who first argued that there are not two but three participants in a supervision session – supervisor, supervisee and service user – each of whom exerts an influence over the discussions which take place. In order to understand how the multitude of functions and tasks of supervision are interrelated and can be successfully managed, Hughes and Pengelly (1997) developed a model based around the connections between two triangles, the first of which (in Figure 9.1) illustrates the presence of the three participants.

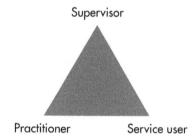

Figure 9.1 The participants in supervision

- *The supervisor*, often (although not always) representing line-management authority and agency accountability.

- *The practitioner*, bringing the results of direct work and evidence-gathering with service users, professionals and other care workers.

- *The service user*, with needs, capacities, demands and rights.

In addition to the three participants, the three key functions of supervision – normative, formative and restorative – can also be represented at each corner of a triangle, as illustrated in Figure 9.2.

Normative
Organisational

Formative   Restorative
Educational   Personal

Figure 9.2 The key functions of supervision

There is a dynamic tension, within and between the corners of the two triangles, as the key relationships and issues involved in any situation present themselves. Although the corners of the two triangles never completely overlap, there are specific connections between the three *functions* of supervision and its three *participants*. To take full account of the complexity of managing all six corners, supervision needs to be 'a flexible space', and the triangle model is particularly helpful if you think of the sides as elastic boundaries, within which the participants can migrate from one corner to another, and functions can be prioritised in different combinations, as discussions about the work develop and progress. These competing tensions will cause the shape of the triangles to change as the priorities ebb and flow. For instance, in the participants' triangle, it may be necessary for both supervisor and practitioner to focus entirely on a service user's rights, at which point all three participants migrate into the service user's corner for a time. Similarly, in the functions triangle, developing a new area of knowledge may emerge as a specific priority, so that the focus will be entirely on the 'educational' corner, with little or no attention paid to the organisational or personal corners for a limited period. The corner that is most likely to be excluded may either be the one which is causing most anxiety to the supervisor or practitioner (Mattinson 1981), or the one to which they have become anxiously attached, unable to risk leaving it for another equally important but less anxiety-provoking corner (Hughes and Pengelly 1997).

Visualising the processes of supervision in this way, and applying the two triangles across the competing tensions of your own work, should help you to:

- keep all three participants and all three functions of supervision in mind, even if the focus on each element is different at any one time

- understand the dynamic interrelationship between the participants and the functions of supervision, and deal with them in a more integrated way, and

- ensure that no corner is ignored or avoided for any length of time.

Making the most of supervision

The work you do and how you do it is at the heart of supervision, and to make the most of what it has to offer, you need to ensure that you take a proactive stance in negotiating what you want and need from supervision. The initial arrangements that you will need to make for supervision were considered as part of the induction processes explored in Chapter 4, including the advantages of developing written agreements, which are increasingly part of agency arrangements for induction and training in the first year in employment.

Expectations, hopes and fears

In a study by Carroll and Gilbert (2005, p.11) a group of supervisees used the following metaphors to describe what supervision meant to them:

- a torch – which illuminates my practice

- a container – where I feel safe and held

- a mirror – where I see myself and my work

- a playpen – where we play with ideas, feelings, intuitions, theories

- a dance – where we learn how to work together in harmony

- a classroom – which contains two learners

- a thermometer – to gauge intellectual, emotional, psychological and social climates

- a sculpture – where I am being fashioned into something yet to be.

You might like to think about what supervision means to you, and begin your first session with your new supervisor by exploring your hopes and fears, and sharing your expectations of a good working alliance. Completing the statements in Box 9.2 about the process, separately from your supervisor, and then comparing responses, could form part of a helpful warm-up exercise.

Box 9.2 Supervision: expectations, hopes and fears

Complete the following statements in relation to your new supervision arrangements, and ask your supervisor to do the same.

- I am expecting supervision to be...

- I am expecting supervision to provide...

- What I fear most in supervision is...

- What I value most in supervision is...

- I hope that supervision will be...

- What interests me about supervision is...

How similar are your responses to those of your supervisor?

What differences are there, and are there any actions you could take, either together or separately, to reduce their impact?

Whatever your hopes and fears, you are not an empty vessel waiting to be filled up, or attempting to become a clone of your supervisor – you will develop your own style and approaches to practice as your experience grows. In Chapter 2, we characterised the development of professional expertise as requiring rather more than an apprenticeship approach, and so it is with supervision, which should enable you to forge your own identity within the overall boundaries of the profession (Carroll and Gilbert 2005). Given that the focus is on your practice and professional development, it is incumbent on you to take whatever action is needed to get what you want and need from supervision.

Channelling your initial enthusiasm appropriately is probably a good place to start. You need to ensure that supervision includes proper development planning, linked to your previous work history, training and placement experiences, and that, in consultation with your supervisor, you use all of this information to set realistic and achievable goals, both in the short term and longer term, that will foster a sense of growth and accomplishment for you. It is here that you should make appropriate links to any formal requirements for NQSWs in the first year in employment which may be part of the CPD framework in the country in which you are practising, as summarised in Chapter 1 (See Table 1.1, page 37). If your initial enthusiasm is not harnessed appropriately, there is a danger that you could be thrown headlong into work in quite an unprotected way, or inadvertently expose yourself to hurt and rejection from service users, leaving you feeling that you are in the wrong job. In order to avoid these sorts of problems, Brown and Bourne (1996) recommend that early supervision sessions should incorporate a 'stress check'.

Stress check

We have earlier argued that a certain amount of stress can be good for you, encouraging you to work at your best without allowing the strains of the job to become overwhelming. The stress check suggested by Brown and Bourne (1996), which is illustrated in Figure 9.3 (page 160), involves mapping the potential and actual stressors that exist within four interconnected systems: your personal life, your practice, your team and the wider organisation in which you are employed.

Figure 9.3 Mapping potential stressors

The four interconnected systems, along with examples of their potential stressors, are as follows:

- *your personal life*: relationship difficulties; illness; financial difficulties; bereavement

- *your practice*: violence; abuse; service users' disclosures; large workload

- *your team*: personal conflicts; bullying; isolation; colleagues' stresses

- *your agency*: new procedures; competition for promotion; reorganisation.

Each stressor can be considered in relation to its impact on you and how you are managing it, and through regular recording and review, any trends that might otherwise not be apparent can be identified. Using this approach to address what might be a sensitive area, early on in supervision, should establish stress management as a central aspect of the routine of supervision discussions, rather than something which is either minimised or ignored all together.

Supervision style
The style in which supervision is both given and received will also be important aspects of the relationship. Heron (1975) divided

any process of facilitation or enabling, of which supervision would certainly be one, into six categories:

- *prescriptive:* giving advice; being directive

- *informative:* being didactic; giving instruction and information

- *confrontative:* challenging; giving direct feedback

- *cathartic:* releasing tension

- *catalytic:* being reflective, encouraging self-directed problem solving

- *supportive:* offering approval, confirmation and validation.

The priority given to each of these categories, and the balance between them, might usefully be the subject of some discussion with your supervisor as you set up your supervision agreement. An exploration of your preferences, and the importance that each of you places on any specific activity, might be helpful in trying to understand and integrate both sides of a healthy 'alliance'.

It is not uncommon to arrive for supervision stressed, anxious, angry or afraid. These feelings are all part of your perceptions of, and responses to, your experiences of work with service users, and interactions with members of your team or the wider organisation in which you are employed. In fact, you might consider that your usual equilibrium and the way in which you normally respond to challenges have been disturbed. This very disturbance to your normal way of being can either generate new energy, which can provide the opportunity for developing more successful ways of dealing with your experiences, or engender feelings of inadequacy and hopelessness, as a precursor to some more defensive or destructive action. Any of the following expressions could indicate that your very 'being' has been challenged (Brown and Bourne 1996, p.119) in a way with which it has been difficult to come to terms:

"Why me?"

"I can't understand it, I thought we had such a good relationship."

"I never believed people could be like that."

"I don't know who I am any longer."

"I can't believe this has happened."

"It feels as though the rug has been pulled from under me."

"I've completely lost it, nothing seems straightforward anymore."

Although perhaps triggered by a particular event, these feelings are more likely to be part of an ongoing process of encountering and attempting to resolve 'crisis situations' which transcend your prior personal and practice experiences. Using crisis intervention theory to shine a light on your own situation might offer you some useful insights into what, in these circumstances, will be most helpful to you in a supervision session. Roberts' (2000) seven stage model of crisis intervention, set out in Table 9.1 outlines a process which is equally applicable to a resolution of your own feelings, including finding support, restoring your confidence and building future resilience.

Table 9.1 Seven stage model of crisis intervention

1. Immediate response

2. Establish rapport

3. Define the major problem

4. Explore feelings

5. Consider alternative responses

6. Make an action plan

7. Review and follow-up support

Source: adapted from Roberts (2000)

The model suggests that when equilibrium is disturbed and usual coping strategies have failed, you need an immediate response. This is where you may need to make use of a manager's open-door policy or other informal arrangements to begin with. Hopefully the rapport you already have with your supervisor will provide the reassurance you need that help is available. You should enter supervision prepared to be open and honest about all of the significant elements of your current situation, and exactly what has brought you to this 'crisis' point. Supervision should provide the safe, understanding and empathic environment in which to express your feelings, but if another setting would be better for you (e.g. a peer support group) then this should be discussed in supervision. Considering alternative responses will involve taking a look, with your supervisor, at your coping strategies and social networks, with a view to suggesting different ways in which you can respond, or different resources on which you can call for support. Any meeting with your supervisor should end with a summary of outcomes, which might include one or two clear goals in relation to your coping strategies.

Meeting arrangements

Over three-quarters of the social workers in our own study identified supervision as one of the most important sources of support, guidance and advice during their first year in employment, but nearly all of them (85%) also reported that insufficient time was allocated to it.

It is not always easy to prioritise supervision in a busy workplace, yet if it is to be given significance and assume its proper importance, arrangements that have been agreed should not be broken lightly, on either side. The knowledge that you can rely on it to be there, without question, is one of the most important understandings that may not actually appear in writing in your supervision agreement. In the early stages of your career you are likely to use supervision as something of a refuge, giving you time to stand back, take stock and restore your equilibrium. If there is any doubt about its availability – that it can be easily brushed aside in favour of competing priorities – then your confidence and self-assurance might easily be undermined or damaged. The firm commitment to regular sessions will help to develop a deeper sense of direction and purpose for supervision as a process of relationship-building, rather than a succession of unconnected encounters for administrative purposes. It is also worth giving some thought to where you will meet, so that it can be somewhere open to least interruptions which can detract from the flow of thoughts and ideas, particularly if you have waited for the right time to broach a more sensitive or difficult subject.

Having agreed on frequency, duration and venue as part of your supervision agreement, it is a good idea to book a programme of meeting dates, possibly for the whole year ahead, in both diaries, to confirm your joint commitment to the arrangements. It is inevitable that, from time to time, other commitments may need to take precedence over supervision, but when any particular session is disrupted in this way, there should be an immediate reminder that a meeting was missed and an alternative date needs to be agreed without delay.

Boundaries

You will already know that all kinds of personal background information can affect your practice as a social worker, and although this does not necessarily entitle your supervisor to information about your personal life, some disclosure is likely to make the relationship more effective. Almost any social work situation has the potential to produce or reproduce personal feelings which need to be shared and explored in order to enable you to practise effectively and maintain your well-being. However, it can feel 'risky' in the early stages of your supervision relationship to disclose personal information or feelings. Setting some boundaries around the supervisory relationship, what is professional and what is personal, should help to clarify matters and create a safe and trusting environment for open discussion. In general, personal material will only be relevant where it is directly affecting the work you are doing, or vice versa. If an initial exploration of personal issues reveals that there are deeper matters than can be met within the bounds of a routine supervision session, then a good supervisor might suggest that they are addressed either in a separate meeting, or perhaps through personal counselling. The latter option may be something which is available within your employing agency, or may require self-referral to another agency. The key message here is that, even if they cannot be resolved in supervision, the importance of these personal feelings should not be ignored or denied.

How you manage the boundaries around confidentiality should also be an important element of the supervision agreement, and the need to be clear about the sort of information that can and cannot be shared, in confidence, is particularly relevant if your supervisor is also your line manager. It is not a good idea to make a tacit assumption that everything said will be treated in confidence, only to find at a later date that confidentiality has been breached. It is therefore better to try to specify in advance what sort of information will need to be taken outside the boundaries of the supervision relationship, together with when, how and to whom it will be taken. Although it will not be possible to cover every eventuality, by being as specific as possible, you minimise the risk of misunderstandings and the possibility of feeling let down or betrayed.

Preparation

Preparation is important, not least because it allows you to play an equal role in setting the agenda and to ensure that you get what you want from supervision. You can also make sure that you address the issues you wish to deal with. Preparation also provides the opportunity to clarify your thinking about all kinds of work-related experiences, not limited only to those which you want to discuss in your next supervision session. Without this more structured approach to your thinking, work can seem like a relentless stream of events, each of which requires your attention before you are confronted by the next one, and so on. It is not always the most obviously important events that are the most productive to deal with in supervision. Sometimes, thinking more broadly around apparently trivial incidents can reveal important insights that would benefit from further discussion. When you are thinking about your practice, there is also a natural tendency to focus on the things that have gone wrong, but it is important that you also remember to reflect on situations that went well, where you feel that you did a piece of really good work, because trying to analyse those situations might also help you to understand better how you can replicate them.

Asking yourself a few questions about your work can be a great help in getting the best out of each supervision session (see Box 9.3, page 166).

Box 9.3 Supervision: preparation questionnaire

As part of your preparation routine for each supervision session, take a few moments to answer the following questions to inform your agenda.

- Which situations do you feel you dealt with well?
- Which did not go so well?
- Were there any situations in which you didn't know what to do?
- Is there any service user relationship or situation which is causing you particular concern?
- Is there any staff relationship – your own team or other professional or agency – which is causing you particular concern?

If you are keeping a reflexive journal, this can be of enormous help in the preparation process. By looking through your journal, you can see whether there are any particular issues or incidents that stand out that you would like to discuss in supervision. You might also identify trends or repeating patterns in your thinking, doing or feeling that would otherwise not be apparent and which it could be important to explore in more detail, with the benefit of your supervisor's perspective.

Your professional development plan should also be a useful source of prompts for supervision, helping you to make the links between current and future types of work – the areas of strength currently being evidenced and the areas for future development, for instance as part of a specific piece of allocated work, or by taking up a shadowing or co-working opportunity, or through specific training. Articulating learning objectives for yourself, as well as in consultation with your supervisor, allows you to develop clear goals towards which you are working, and which can also be linked to more formal NQSW/ASYE requirements. Your supervisor can help you monitor your progress and provide ongoing feedback as well as evidence for assessment of consolidation and development of knowledge and skills. If it makes a regular appearance in supervision sessions in this way, your professional development plan will ensure that professional development has its proper place on the agenda.

Talking and listening

Talking and listening are probably the key interpersonal skills that are the foundation of your social work practice, and they are no less central to developing a trusting, open and honest relationship within supervision. To get the best out of supervision, you need to pay attention both to what you say and to what is said to you.

First, when you set out to describe a situation, try to be as concise as possible, keeping to the point and providing only the details that are necessary to provide an appropriate overview for your supervisor. This will maximise the time available for you to go through the important issues thoroughly. Guard against any tendency to occupy the time in supervision with every single detail of a case as a defence or avoidance mechanism, thereby preventing the central difficulties and dilemmas being brought out into the open for discussion.

As already noted, you should try to contribute positive as well as negative material to supervision. There can be as much benefit to your learning from analysing a situation that went well as from discussing something that didn't. A good supervisor will want to 'establish an atmosphere of competence' (Morrison 2001) by eliciting from you some of the pieces of work that have gone well and produced positive outcomes, however small those may have been, before you discuss any problems. Without this sort of structure, there is a real danger that supervision can become overburdened with problems, focusing exclusively on risks, weaknesses, failings and limitations, thereby undermining your confidence and tending to magnify feelings of confusion or inadequacy which are common for any new member of staff.

Supervision is of course a dialogue, a two-way process, within which it is surprisingly easy for people to misunderstand each other. Reflecting back what has been said to you is a skill that you will regularly use with service users, and this same skill can be equally helpful in making sure that you have understood (and not distorted) what has been said in supervision. Paraphrasing or making a short summary, reflected back to your supervisor, will allow you to correct any misunderstandings and clarify decisions and plans for action which can then be accurately recorded.

Feedback and criticism

An important part of the dialogue in supervision will be giving and receiving feedback. Again, the general 'rules' for giving feedback will be familiar to you from your direct work with service users, but here too it might be helpful to consider these in relation to your supervision. Good feedback should be clear, owned, regular, balanced and specific. If it is not, you can ask for clarification – you do not have to be a passive recipient in the process. Try to receive others' feedback as *their* experiences of you, in which it is often sufficient to hear and simply acknowledge what has been said. It is quite common in the early stages of a career to feel that any difficulties are the equivalent of personal failings which reflect directly on your competence and suitability, rather than challenges which, in time, you will successfully overcome. Difficulties can arise if you react immediately to perceived criticism, without taking the time to listen properly to what was actually said. Careful listening is required, even in uncomfortable circumstances, in which you take time to think things through. Try not to automatically agree or disagree, or compulsively to explain. The skill here is in recognising when to be assertive and when it is more appropriate to take time to reflect on what you have heard. Everybody makes mistakes or fails to meet the standard that they would ideally like to meet from time to time. Judging yourself too harshly can mean that you shut down and block out what happened, rather than being open to discussion and learning from it. Occasionally, you may find that something you felt was reasonable at the time, later evokes strong emotions. Delayed reactions of this sort are not uncommon, and you may find it helpful to discuss these feelings and their causes with your supervisor at your next meeting. If you do not raise them, your supervisor will have no way of knowing how you felt, and keeping them to yourself can easily build up resentment which will doubtless emerge to cause problems later. Of course, all of this requires a measure of courage on your part, as well as trust in your supervisor. Usually, trust comes with knowing your supervisor well, which takes time, but building a more trusting relationship will enable you to start letting go of defensive feelings and to begin to discuss important issues more freely, without feeling that you are being judged.

Blocks

The learning function of supervision draws heavily on the reflection-action model which may be familiar to you from the four stages of Kolb's experiential learning cycle, set out in Figure 9.4.

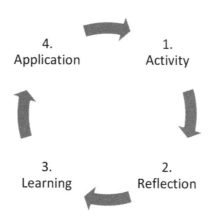

Figure 9.4 Four stages of the experiential learning cycle (adapted from Kolb 1984)

Although you would normally expect to be moving smoothly through each stage of the cycle as you develop your professional practice, it is quite possible that, at times, you may find yourself 'stuck' at a particular stage. For example, you may become so stressed with a heavy workload that you are unable to do your work in the way you would like, to meet the standards that you expect from yourself, so that you are stuck in Stage 1, or you may be so worried about getting it right and proving yourself in a new job that you shut down reflection by excluding any reference to areas that are not going well, becoming stuck in Stage 2. Alternatively, you may feel that it is too risky to admit to not knowing something and avoid asking for the help that you need, so that learning fails to occur (Stage 3), or you may be tempted to take on too much, too quickly, and in a whirlwind of frenetic activity, allow yourself no time to consider changes and apply what you have learned (Stage 4). It is possible to become stuck in the learning cycle at any stage in your professional development, and if you recognise any of these blocks to progression, you should consider discussing your thoughts and feelings in supervision. Framing the difficulty in terms of a block in the learning cycle may make it easier for you to initiate discussion in order to find the help that will, in Kadushin's words, 'comfort, bolster and refresh your certainty and conviction' (Kadushin 1976, p.229).

Recording

Your supervision agreement should include a section about how the sessions are to be recorded. The written record will allow you to review what happened and provide you with a summary of what was agreed. Without a signed written record, it may be difficult to refer back with certainty at a later date to a specific agreed action or outcome, as a social worker in one of our studies put it:

> Well, if it isn't written here, then it didn't happen. (Social worker)

A useful format for supervision notes (Carroll and Gilbert 2005) might include the headings set out in Table 9.2.

Table 9.2 Supervision notes: format

Issues raised in this session	
Client issues	Intervention issues
Supervisee issues	Supervisor issues
Organisational issues	Learning objectives/training issues
Action points	
Signatures	

When you come to prepare for the next session, notes of the previous session will be helpful to keep track of the key action points and how your practice has developed. You can use your supervision notes to pick up any key concepts, and indicate how, when and where you have applied them. These are the key skills of critical analysis and reflection, and used in this way they should become integrated into your day-to-day practice, and might also make a useful adjunct to your reflexive journal, allowing you to take a proactive role in summarising your learning in a more global way. There is more about critical reflection in Chapter 12, but supervision is crucially important in providing you with an opportunity to reflect critically on your practice, to share and gain feedback on your insights and ideas, enabling you to develop in confidence and ability as a social worker.

Limits

It has been shown (Rauktis and Koeske 1994) that supportive supervision has a consistently positive effect on job satisfaction, bolstering the psychological and interpersonal resources that enable you to cope and deliver effective job performance for the benefit of service users. This process is represented in Figure 9.5.

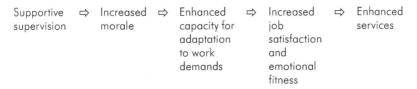

Figure 9.5 Impact of supportive supervision on job satisfaction

There is, however, one important limiting factor to bear in mind. When work demands are high, emotionally supportive supervision loses some of its benefits. Even supportive supervision cannot overcome a work environment in which demands have become excessive. You, your supervisor and your employing agency must be aware of these constraints, recognising the point when altering work demands is the only appropriate response to ensure that you can maintain your well-being, morale and effectiveness. If this point is not recognised by others, you might need to take the lead in supervision discussions, suggesting appropriate amendments, as the NQSW quoted here did:

> I went to my boss and said 'Look, I can't cope this with any more. You've got to tell me how to sort this out.' ...So we broke it down and said this is what we need to do. So it became a very practical task and that helped. (NQSW)

Other suggestions that you could take to supervision when workload demands are outstripping your capacity to cope might include some of the following:

- sorting out priorities for individual cases or tasks

- agreeing a temporary reduction in your overall caseload

- reviewing and adjusting previously agreed deadlines or timetables

- sharing responsibility (e.g. with a co-worker or supervisor) for complex pieces of work/decisions

- achieving a better balance of work (e.g. including some less problematic cases)

- weaving some training into your diary.

Managing the tensions in supervision
Previous experiences
Previous experiences of supervision can have a strong influence on your current attitudes and how well you feel the purposes of supervision are being met. A bad experience can make you wary of entering into another potentially unsatisfactory situation. On the other hand, a really good experience can make you apprehensive that any new arrangements will not match up to the standard that you've come to expect and rely on.

Receiving support
Receiving support is an area to which social workers can sometimes apply double standards, preferring the relative safety of the provider role. While people who use services are encouraged to identify their needs (as well as their strengths), there is a tendency, widely reinforced in the culture of some workplaces, to deny your own needs on the grounds that you should be able to cope and that to have needs implies weakness or dependency. The importance of guarding against the tendency to use supervision as a process only for dealing with problems was considered in Chapter 4, but it is significant enough to warrant reiteration here.

Defensive routines

Personal inhibition and defensive reactions can be major impediments to the establishment of a supportive supervisory alliance. Have you ever found yourself saying, thinking or feeling some of the following defensive routines (Hawkins and Shohet 2006)?

"Yes, yes, I've already thought of that."

"I'll just keep talking, and give you every single detail."

"It's all done and dusted – no problems. All finished."

"I know I've made a mess with this one."

"I know you're not going to be very happy with this but…"

The focused, one-to-one attention in supervision can often feel like scrutiny, in which you are very much on the spot. This was memorably expressed, by one NQSW in our research, as 'snoopervision':

> It's an interesting one because the pressures that are being put on managers are such that supervision is changing from supervision to 'snoopervision' to coin a phrase, and our managers are now required to do two file audits every supervision to check that you've got all the documents in there, and that they are up to date and in the right sections. (NQSW)

Conflict of roles

With managers required to look for administrative compliance at the same time as social workers are seeking support and guidance, there can be an inherent mismatch of expectations from supervision. Furthermore, as the following comments from supervisors illustrate, managers are often doing their job with very little specific training or preparation for their role:

> It sounds a bit negative but yes, that was my experience… [when I was promoted]…you get a new office and you just get on with it.

The training courses that are set up often don't meet the need because they're too late and they're not directed at what you're doing.

I don't think there is a very good programme really for managers – one minute you're a social worker and the next minute you're a manager and you're just expected to get on with it and you apply, well it's a bit how you learn to be a parent really, you come through by osmosis and you've been working for a manager and you probably try and apply what you consider to be the best from what you've experienced. (First line managers in statutory agencies)

Shared 'interprofessional' supervision

Multidisciplinary teams, for example hospital discharge, community mental health, assertive outreach, crisis intervention and home treatment teams, commonly bring together a range of different professionals, such as nurses, occupational therapists, clinical psychologists and psychiatrists, as well as social workers, and it is not uncommon for social workers to be supervised by a line manager who is not a registered social worker.

While this may offer insights into different perspectives on practice, there is a risk that supervision from a person outside of your own profession may contribute to an early loss of professional identity and confidence in your own role. Your line manager will hold ultimate responsibility for providing you with access to high-quality supervision, but need not necessarily deliver every function themselves, and in multidisciplinary settings 'line management' is frequently separated from 'professional' supervision provided by someone from your own profession. Where more than one person is providing different aspects of your supervision, it is essential that everyone involved is clear about their respective roles and responsibilities. As a starting point, Table 9.3 suggests some of the areas which it might be helpful for you to clarify if you have more than one supervisor.

Table 9.3 Shared responsibilities: clarifying line management and professional supervision

Responsibilities	Line manager	Professional supervisor
Performance management		
Agreeing and monitoring outcomes		
Specialist/case supervision		
Identifying CPD and learning needs		
Meeting CPD and learning needs		
Complex practice issues e.g. safeguarding		
Appraisal		
Interagency working		
Reflective and evidence-based practice		
Emotional issues and support		
Workload management		
Feedback on performance		
Feedback on practice		
Conditions of service issues		
Other		

Source: adapted from Children's Workforce Development Council (CWDC 2009)

In addition, you might also like to include answers to the following questions in your supervision agreement (see Chapter 5):

- Are timings between sessions with each supervisor clear and reasonable?

- Are supervision notes shared?

- Are there opportunities for occasional joint three-way meetings?

If there is an expectation that you will be supervised by your line manager, who is from a different professional background, and you are not offered some degree of formal support from a registered social worker, it may be helpful to discuss the issue of professional identity with your supervisor. It may also be useful to explore other sources of professional support that may be available to you, such as NQSW support groups or learning sets, special interest group meetings or online forums and networks.

Evaluation

We began the chapter by emphasising the centrality of learning to the supervision process and the two-way nature of a successful alliance between supervisee and supervisor. Taking this to its logical conclusion, and bringing both aspects together, 'learning from the learning' will be maximised where there are regular and structured opportunities for honest and open reflection built into the processes, to complete a feedback cycle for both parties to the supervision agreement.

As you settle into your supervision arrangements, you and your supervisor might like to evaluate how well a particular supervision session has gone by answering the following questions:

- What went particularly well/badly in this session?

- Were we communicating effectively with each other?

- What did we not talk about, and why?

- What, if any, external factors affected the session?

- What three actions could improve the quality of future sessions?

(adapted from Carroll and Gilbert 2005)

An alternative approach would be to complete the questionnaire below (which is phrased as though from your supervisor, in order to provide an opportunity for feedback from you as supervisee) at some time during your first year in post.

- Am I providing the sort of supervision you need?

- Is the supervision relationship productive? Anything we need to discuss?

- Is the feedback I give clear, regular, balanced and specific enough?

- Is there a good balance of support and challenge in our supervision?

- Are there areas that we do not talk about that should be the focus of a conversation?

- Do our discussions make an impact on your practice?

- What seems to you to be the next challenge in your development?

- What is most helpful about our supervision arrangement? What least helpful?

- Is there anything that you would like me to stop doing? Start doing? Increase? Decrease?

- Are we being accountable in our supervision? To service users? To the organisation? To the profession?

(adapted from Carroll and Gilbert 2005)

Key considerations for making the most of supervision

- There are three 'participants' in supervision (social worker; supervisor; service user) and three broad functions (organisational; educational; personal), all of which need to be kept in mind.

- Supervision is identified as one of the most important sources of support and guidance by NQSWs, but the majority also report that insufficient time is allocated to it, so ensure that you and your supervisor give it the priority that it deserves.

- Supervision is likely to be most effective when you play an active part in setting the agenda and prepare properly for each session. The more you put into your supervision, the more you are likely to get out of it.

- Remember that supervision, on its own, also has its limits – if the work demands being placed on you are simply too great, you need to do something to change your workload rather than just talking about the effect it is having on you (and your service users).

Additional Resources

Further reading

Article describing 'critical ingredients for effective supervision' and introducing a '4x4x4' integrated model of supervision.

Supervision: Now or Never − Reclaiming Reflective Supervision in Social Work, Morrison, T. and Wonnacott J., (2010): www.in-trac.co.uk/supervision-now-or-never.

Expectations of service users and carers

Working Towards Person-Centred Support: A Local Case Study. Postle, K., Croft, S., Fleming, J., Beresford, P., Bewley, C., Branfield, F., and Glynn, M. (2011). Produced by The Standards We Expect Project/Shaping Our Lives/Joseph Rowntree Foundation: www.shapingourlives.org.uk/documents/SWEx_CaseStudy.pdf.

Scotland

A prompt or tool which employers and practitioners can use to assess whether the appropriate conditions are met to ensure safe and effective practice.

Guidance, Consultation and Supervision − Key Area 4 in Practice Governance Framework: Responsibility and Accountability in Social Work Practice (Scottish Government 2011): www.scotland.gov.uk/Publications/2011/03/24111247/6.

Guidance linking supervision to the consolidation of social work skills, knowledge and values in the first 12 months of entry to the social work register.

The Role of Supervision in PRTL, p.11 in Guidance Notes for NQSWs − Post registration Training and Learning Requirements for Newly qualified Social Workers (SSSC 2011): www.sssc.uk.com/Already-registered/post-registration-training-and-learning-prtl-for-newly-qualified-social-workers-nqsw.html.

Wales
Guidance for establishing an individual development plan including arrangements for supervision, as part of a structured approach to the first year in practice.
Making the Most of the First Year in Practice: A Guide for Newly Qualified Social Workers (CCW 2008) beta.scie-socialcareonline.org.uk/making-the-most-of-the-first-year-in-practice-a-guide-for-newly-qualified-social-workers/r/a11G00000017vHflAI.

Guidance on new arrangements for social work career pathways including supervision contracts.
Supporting NQSWs in Wales: Arrangements for 2013 and Beyond (CCW 2013): www.ccwales.org.uk/post-qualifying-training/.

Guidance setting out what is expected of social workers, supporting best practice, based around the National Occupational Standards: www.ccwales.org.uk/practice-guidance-for-social-workers.
Supervision and reflection – Para. 29 in The Social Worker: Practice Guidance for Social Workers Registered with the Care Council for Wales (CCW 2014).

Northern Ireland
Guidance specifying minimum requirements of employers and social workers in relation to supervision for AYE pp.5–6.
The Assessed year in Employment (AYE) for Newly qualified Social Workers in NI (NISCC 2010): www.niscc.info/files/201405_AYE GuidanceForRegistrantsAndEmployers_Publication_MAY2014V1_JH.pdf.

England
Guidance on expectations for supervision and reflection linked to a written learning agreement.
The Social Work ASYE: A Mini-Guide to the Assessed and Supported Year in Employment Section 7: The S in ASYE Stands for 'Supported' (Skills for Care 2012): www.skillsforcare.org.uk/Document-library/Social-work/Support-and-assessment/ASYE-mini-guide-Jan-14.pdf.

Going the Distance

- ❖ Chapter 10 Dealing with stress, emotion and exhaustion
- ❖ Chapter 11 Working in a satisfying climate
- ❖ Chapter 12 Managing increasing complexity

As your day-to-day practice becomes more streamlined and you deal more confidently with the range of tasks allocated to you, this final part of the book considers the influence of your employing organisation on you and, conversely, how you can begin to have some influence on the organisation. This part aims to help you develop a better understanding of how your own position, practice and role 'fit' within the overall organisation, taking account of three primary aspects – structure, culture and climate – which together are likely to have a significant impact on your experience of the organisation and the quality of your working life.

Chapter 10 explores a range of demands, constraints and personal traits affecting workplace stress and job satisfaction, as well as identifying helpful strategies and positive coping mechanisms. Stress is not always a bad thing. Some degree of stress can be good for you in providing motivation to achieve things which you might have thought were out of reach.

Chapter 11 returns to look again at the team and teamwork as we consider your development as an 'effective operator' within your organisational context.

Chapter 12 explores some of the links between critical reflection, reflective practice and learning organisations. Some of these ideas take us back to the discussions about the development of professional expertise in Chapter 2, as you move on in your practice, absorbing new and more challenging experiences and working with greater complexity and increasing uncertainty.

Chapter 10

Dealing with Stress, Emotion and Exhaustion

- Identifying stressors
- Negative consequences of stress
- Coping mechanisms
- Key considerations in dealing with stress, emotion and exhaustion

Stress is experienced subjectively, with individuals reacting in very different ways to the same situation (Storey and Billingham 2001). While a certain amount of stress can be good for you, too much can produce tension, anxiety and depression. As the following quotes illustrate, stress has been recognised as a serious problem in the workplace for many years:

> Overwork can kill…especially if combined with high demand, low control and poor social support… job strain predicted mortality. (Michie and Cockcroft 1996, p.921)

> Stress is still the biggest problem in UK workplaces with excessive workloads, job cuts and rapid change the most common triggers for rising stress levels among employees… stress is the greatest cause of absence from work. (TUC 2006)

Numerous studies and reports have concluded that social work is an extremely demanding job. As far back as 1980, Maslach demonstrated that factors intrinsic to the job, rather than the personality of those engaged in doing it, are highly related to burnout (Maslach 1980). Managing stress at work therefore needs to begin with a clear acknowledgement that stress is an organisational concern rather than an individual failing (Thompson *et al.* 1996).

There is more about the effects of organisational culture on social workers in Chapter 11, but in this chapter we focus in more detail on what causes stress and the steps you can take to deal with its negative consequences by developing effective coping mechanisms.

Identifying stressors

To help you make sense of some of the ideas in this chapter, and to apply them to your own work situation, you might find it helpful to answer the following questions before reading the rest of the chapter.

Box 10.1 How do you work with stressful situations?
PART 1: IDENTIFYING STRESSORS
Call to mind a challenging situation you have dealt with at work involving service users, managers, colleagues or other professionals.

Jot down some of your thoughts in answer to the following questions:

- What happened?
- What were the most upsetting aspects?
- What impact did the experience have on you at the time?
- What were the longer term effects of the experience?

Stress occurs when there is a lack of balance in the demands and constraints placed on a person in relation to the internal and external supports available to them (Jones, Fletcher and Ibbetson 1991). This definition is helpful in three ways: first, because it introduces the important idea of bringing competing demands into some sort of balance; second, because it emphasises that stress is not a static state but a dynamic one involving three key elements – demands, constraints and support; and third, because it makes reference to 'internal supports', alerting us to the role of personal characteristics.

Several disciplines have developed models of stress, with those that reflect the dynamic interrelationship of a range of different factors being the most helpful in trying to understand occupational or work-related stress in a range of social work settings (Karasek 1979; Lazarus and Folkman 1984). The domains affecting workplace stress and job satisfaction – demands, constraints and personal traits – are presented in Figure 10.1 along each of the three sides of a triangle, enabling the interactions between different factors within each domain, particular to social work, to be analysed.

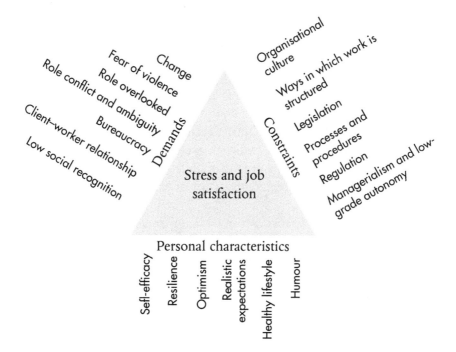

Figure 10.1 The interaction of demands, constraints and personal traits in stress and job satisfaction

A large number of studies have shown that high demands in a job may not be stressful if there are low constraints, good levels of support and high levels of control and autonomy (e.g. Collins 2007; Jenaro, Flores and Arias 2007; Morris 2005). Increased support and self-efficacy help to reduce feelings of stress, even though the demands of the job may be high.

Demands

The factors presented along this side of the triangle are all frequently identified demands of the job, and they can provoke feelings of stress, anxiety and exhaustion.

> This is so different from the job I expected. This isn't what I was trained to do at all. (NQSW)

> I still wake up sometimes at 2 a.m. in the morning and start thinking about cases, worrying about stuff, did I do this, should I have done that, if I'd done this differently would that have had a better outcome, especially with cases that I don't feel completely at ease about. (NQSW)

In response to frequent policy developments and new government initiatives, social work agencies nowadays are engaged in an almost continual process of *change*. Opportunities abound, but not without a good deal of uncertainty, which is well documented as a source of workplace stress. This means that skills in managing change are becoming almost core requirements for anyone entering the social work profession.

Actual or threatened *violence* is another important cause of stress in the everyday working lives of social workers (Smith and Nursten 1998), with particular implications here for lone working. For example, following the Baby P case in Haringey, a Unison ten-point plan called for all child-protection investigation visits to be conducted by *two* practitioners, each with at least two years' post-qualifying experience (Community Care 2008).

Overload refers to feelings of being overwhelmed – either by having too much to do and too little time in which to do it, or by the allocation of tasks which are beyond your present level of confidence, ability or training. The Social Work Task Force in England reported that 'too many social workers are carrying caseloads which can be too high' and noted the detrimental effects this could have on morale, health and well-being (SWTF 2009a, p.29). Overload was reported as a common experience by the NQSWs in our own research.

> And you know, when you're carrying a caseload of 18, 20,
> 22, I would just cancel supervision just to get work done.
> (NQSW)

> And I mean at my highest, I was carrying 22 when I was newly
> qualified with 8 of those being child protection. (Social worker,
> 9 months post-qualification)

The Social Work Task Force went on to suggest that a whole systems approach to managing all of the pressures on workload, rather than simply attending to a single *numerical* caseload limit, was what was needed. However, it is generally accepted that developing a caseload management system is a very complex task, with different models based variously on time, points awarded for 'standard' cases, or tasks/pieces of work used as the base unit, rather than cases (SWTF 2009b). The variety of social work roles and settings, the complexity of circumstances being addressed, and the need to respond to unforeseen events require a high degree of flexibility, so that caseload management in social work can never be an exact science. However, in recognition of the part played by workload issues in retaining social workers at the frontline, and the expectation that employers should make use of effective workforce planning and implement transparent systems to manage workload and case allocation (SWRB 2010), recent attempts have been made across the UK to provide a range of models, toolkits and practice templates to assist managers in the process of establishing equitable and manageable caseloads for their staff (see 'Additional Resources' for further details of different UK models). It is important for you to raise any serious concerns that you have about workload issues as soon as possible in supervision, as well as more broadly within the team in which you are working. Help in saying no could be useful in this regard (see Chapter 7).

Role conflict and ambiguity arise in circumstances where your own beliefs and values are either incompatible with those of the organisation in which you are working, or where there are unclear boundaries and lines of accountability in relation to your duties and responsibilities. Where these issues exist they may also need to be discussed in supervision, or with members of the team in which you are working. *Bureaucracy* is often experienced as a rising tide of paperwork, complex forms, problematic IT systems and performance management processes. These have become persistent sources of pressure, frustration and stress for many social workers (see Chapter 6 for ideas about dealing with the bureaucratic burden).

The sensitivity and responsiveness needed to deal with the difficult range of problems that can be presented by *client–worker relationships* potentially expose social workers to particularly stressful situations (Bennett, Evans and Tattersall 1993). For example, restricted resources often lead to perceptions of having made an inadequate response to service user needs, because the only choices for action appear to be between several equally unsatisfactory alternatives. This can combine with the *low social recognition* and poor regard for the profession which are frequently identified by social workers as another source of stress. In particular, following child abuse tragedies or reports into failures to safeguard vulnerable adults or protect the public, negative media portrayals and political criticism of social work can produce feelings of being undervalued and misunderstood compared to other helping professions.

Constraints

Factors which limit or constrain the autonomy and decision-making of social workers are gathered together along the right-hand side of the triangle. The *culture of the organisation* in which you are employed is perhaps the most significant constraining influence. The layers of responsibility within an organisational structure can serve to frustrate attempts to make speedy, sensible decisions at the frontline, and when decisions have been made, a blame culture can leave you feeling persecuted and alone when problems arise.

The *ways in which work is structured* can also impose significant constraints on your practice (Stevenson 1981). For example, current trends towards a greater number of 'specialist' teams and the contracting out of services can result in unhelpful fragmentation of knowledge, skills and resources. Despite the fact that repeated change of their social worker is cited as a key concern by children and young people as well as those using adult services (Beresford 2012; Morgan 2006), organisational imperatives often mean that you have little control over the length of your involvement with particular service users. The associated lack of continuity is likely to have a detrimental effect, not only on the service user concerned, but also on your own sense of achievement and self-efficacy.

Legislation and regulation can also present major constraints on your practice, often limiting individual creativity and professional autonomy. For example, all social work agencies are regulated and have to be accountable for their performance, which requires that ever-increasing amounts of data are collected, often using tick-box forms that have to be completed by practitioners and managers within set deadlines. *Managerialism* has flourished in such a climate, with bureaucratic approaches to the allocation and measurement of workloads, for example, having taken hold across almost all social work organisations. While most social workers recognise the pressures on managers to set and meet performance targets, it has been shown that the pressure involved in planning and meeting these kinds of deadlines is a strong predictor of overall stress for those delivering frontline services (Morris 2005).

Personal characteristics

Clearly, some of the demands and constraints considered above will be more readily amenable to individual control than others, so we now go on to consider the personal characteristics which have been shown to have a moderating effect on the experience of occupational stress.

Self-efficacy, which in this context is the belief in your own capability to organise and carry out a course of action successfully to perform your job, is one of the variables which plays an important part in the relationship between demands, constraints and job satisfaction. For example, there is evidence of a direct relationship between high levels of self-efficacy and increased learning, persistence and job performance in complex situations (Jimmieson 2000). *Resilience* also plays a part in determining how individual workers respond to different experiences, although it needs to be recognised that resilience is not simply a personal characteristic as it is influenced by the context and the culture of the organisation in which you are working, which can facilitate or hinder the development of your ability to 'bounce back' from negative emotional experiences (Beddoe, Davys and Adamson 2011; Grant and Kinman 2012). While many social work methods are based on the central importance of relationships and emotion, it is somewhat ironic that many social workers are expected to undertake their work in bureaucratic organisations dominated by structures, procedures and rules which largely ignore personal emotion, treating staff more or less as 'technical operatives', and offering them little professional autonomy in the performance of their roles.

Optimism is another important characteristic that makes a healthy contribution to the ability to bounce back and sustain a positive psychological state and good self-esteem (Dekel *et al.* 2006). It may either be expressed as a global expectation that good things will be plentiful in the future and bad things scarce, or as an explanatory style which blames external factors for bad events, identifying specific causes and how these might be changed. By contrast, the explanatory style of a pessimist will favour internal, long-lasting and all-pervasive personal causes, which cannot be changed, for any problems which arise (Collins 2007). These concepts lean heavily on the early work of Seligman (1975) about 'learned helplessness', which proposed that, after experiencing uncontrollable events, people become unresponsive and passive through a learned general expectancy that future outcomes will be unrelated to their own actions. It may be worth noting that Seligman later reframed these explanatory styles in terms of 'learned optimism' (2006), based on the ability to frame stressful situations as challenges offering potential benefits and opportunities. However, it is also important to *retain realistic expectations*. Taking a relentlessly optimistic approach can lead you into pursuing unachievable goals or striving for control over events without taking proper account of the constraints involved. Optimism must therefore be used as a flexible response, in appropriate circumstances, rather than as a habitual reflex, regardless of context. The greatest value of optimism is that it encourages a focus on strengths, which should underpin any work with service users.

As discussed in Chapter 7, a *healthy lifestyle*, particularly involving exercise and other positive activities, can also be an effective means of coping and improving stress management, while an unhealthy lifestyle can increase the negative effects of workplace stress. Although it has been noted that those (especially women) constrained by other demands, such as family care-giving activities, are more likely to have less energy and time to exercise (Burton and Turrell 2000), a study in Finland found that women employed in the public sector who took regular physical exercise were more satisfied with combining their job and family responsibilities (Kouvonen *et al.* 2005).

The final personal characteristic considered along the bottom of the triangle is *a sense of humour.* Cited as a requirement in so many recruitment advertisements, humour applied to social work can be a controversial topic. The sensitivity of a particular situation may not call for humour, and sometimes there may simply be no funny side to things. However, it has been shown that a sense of humour can mitigate the effects of stress, producing the same kinds of calm, positive well-being and health benefits known to be associated with exercise and relaxation (Martin 2001). For example, in a study involving focus group discussions with informal carers conducted by one of the authors, participants frequently commented on the value of 'being able to laugh' in the face of difficult and challenging situations, providing a release for emotion that might otherwise be unbearable. Laughing at one's own difficult situations in this way, often referred to as 'gallows humour', seems to bring a sense of control to situations which are largely uncontrollable, and is self-affirming as well as promoting bonding and support, as it did for these carers. In this context, it is interesting to note that a study of social work students (Moran and Hughes 2006) found that they scored lower than average for their sense of humour, which may indicate that encouragement and 'permission' from colleagues, supervisors and managers to use humour as an appropriate coping mechanism, may be needed before social workers feel free to draw on its potential benefits.

Negative consequences of stress

While stress does not result in serious ill health for most, the 'ripple effect' on others in the workplace and on the work or service offered, can be considerable, especially over time. We noted at the beginning of this chapter that an optimum level of stress can be good for you, acting as a positive motivational incentive to achieve things that might not otherwise be possible. Stress becomes harmful, however, when there is a loss of balance between what is being demanded of you and the resources available to you to meet those demands, and can result in poor decision-making, presenteeism, or absenteeism, and burnout.

Poor decision-making

When stress is too challenging, rather than you enjoying and developing through your work experiences, just surviving them becomes the major imperative, and your usual behaviour may begin to alter. You might experience any (or all) of the following:

- loss of concentration

- an inability to handle new information

- an increased tendency to procrastinate or postpone activities

- hasty decision-making or 'panicked' choices

- oversimplification of alternatives

- a reduction in creative thinking

- more defensiveness about your decisions

- more irrational or hostile feelings

- increasing withdrawal and social isolation.

In these circumstances, the quality of decision-making becomes diminished and more 'risky', with potentially serious implications (Morris 2005). There is growing evidence of an inability to handle new information and to hold a more defensive decision-making position among stressed social workers. For example, a Canadian study of child protection workers found that, among those who decided there was no risk to the child in a case of chronic neglect, higher stress scores predicted making this decision early and holding it with greater certainty (McGee 1989).

Presenteeism and absenteeism

Presenteeism, a word coined in 2001 by Cary Cooper, Professor of Organisational Psychology and Health at Manchester University, refers to the inappropriate non-use of sick leave, which is a growing concern in many workplaces, where it is associated with increasing levels of stress. It can be difficult to disclose stress in an organisational culture where it is viewed as a sign of individual weakness. Fear of blame, a misplaced commitment to service users and colleagues, or worries about jeopardising progression and promotion by having a poor attendance record sometimes seem compelling reasons to remain at work when really you should be at home because of illness. Where presenteeism exists, short-term absences may well be low, but longer absences may increase due to the eventual onset of more serious physical or psychological illness. The irony, here, is that working in an organisation beset by longer term *absenteeism* actually increases the stresses experienced by those remaining at work, leading to yet more absences and associated difficulties with staff recruitment and retention. In these circumstances your morale, as well as arrangements for your ongoing supervision, support and development, are bound to be jeopardised. Before applying for or accepting a new post, it could be worth looking at vacancy rates to get an understanding of which employers are performing better in this regard. In England, social worker vacancy rates are published, for both adults' and children's services, as part of the National Minimum Data Set, on the Skills for Care website.[2]

Burnout

Burnout is the final consequence of chronic, unalleviated work stress, and studies have shown that there is a high incidence of burnout among social workers, for example those who provide care to children at risk (McGee 1989). The risks and perils of burnout should not be underestimated, and you would do well to remain vigilant on your own behalf, as well as colleagues'. Burnout combines feelings of emotional exhaustion with negative attitudes towards the employing organisation and colleagues, and the depersonalisation of service users (Maslach and Leiter 1997).

Figure 10.2 (page 194) summarises the major factors associated with burnout, presenting the balance that exists between the demands of your job and the level of control you feel you have (four quadrants), and their related impacts on professional development and job satisfaction (rectangular boxes). On each side of the circle, a level of support, either high or low, has been added to the critical factors influencing positive development or burnout. Since individual variables, such as coping strategies and job satisfaction, account for only one-fifth of the symptoms of burnout (Jenaro *et al.* 2007), careful attention needs to be paid to external factors.

---

2   See www.skillsforcare.org.uk for more information.

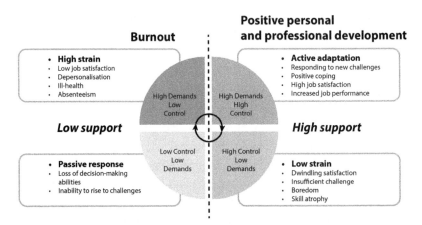

Figure 10.2 Conditions for burnout (adapted from Karasek 1979)

The single most important buffer against stress and burnout cited by social workers, not only in our own research but in a number of other studies (e.g. Bednar 2003; Collins 2007; Stalker *et al.* 2007; Takeda *et al.* 2005), is seeking and finding support from a wide range of sources, which is the focus of Chapter 8.

Coping mechanisms

At the beginning of this chapter we identified that stress is an almost inevitable aspect of social work, arising from the interplay between personal, structural and organisational factors intrinsic to the job. So how do you cope – modifying and adapting your behaviour to meet the demands of the job? (see Box 10.2).

Box 10.2 How do you work with stressful situations?

PART 2: USING INTERNAL AND EXTERNAL RESOURCES

Reflect in a bit more depth on your experiences of the situation that you identified at the beginning of the chapter.

- What coping mechanisms, if any, did you employ to deal with the stresses you encountered?

- What influenced your choice?

- Did you consider any alternative strategies?

Coping mechanisms are crucial in helping you to deal with stressful situations at work. Coping can involve either taking action when something constructive can be done to alter the cause of the stress (i.e. problem-focused), or it can be aimed at reducing or managing the distress you are experiencing when the cause of the stress is outside your control (i.e. emotion-focused). It is instructive to look at some unhelpful responses first, before going on to consider a range of helpful coping strategies.

Unhelpful strategies

There are a number of largely unhelpful ways of trying to deal with stress at work. Among the most common are the four 'Ds' – diversion, disengagement, denial and depersonalisation. *Diversion* involves directing attention elsewhere, for instance by inappropriate use of sick leave or even handing in an abrupt resignation, while *disengagement* can take one of two forms. The first, known as behavioural disengagement or self-blaming, involves marginalising the part that you feel you can play in determining your circumstances, thereby reducing your efforts and effectively giving up. This attitude has close links with the learned helplessness described by Seligman (1975). The other form is mental disengagement, which involves escape or avoidance. This takes over when you distance yourself from thinking about behavioural responses to a demanding situation. It may present itself in a range of activities, such as wishful thinking, daydreaming, excessive sleeping, or the misuse of alcohol and drugs.

Denial is a form of coping involving a refusal to believe that a stressor exists. It has links with pessimism, and an excessive focus on emotional distress and disengagement. Rather worryingly, a study of coping styles by Fineman (1985) found that the internalisation of difficulties, allowing them to build up in the hope that they will disappear or be released elsewhere, was the most dominant coping style used by social workers at that time. And finally, *depersonalisation* can be thought of as a coping strategy that is neither problem-focused nor emotion-focused, characterised by negative, cynical or impersonal feelings towards those who use services, and is often the ultimate response of someone working in an environment which they perceive as hostile, when all other strategies do not seem to work any longer. It is used to avoid experiencing severe levels of emotional exhaustion, and can be a forerunner of more serious burnout.

Helpful strategies

More helpful coping strategies include acceptance, balanced expectations, positive reappraisal, rehearsal, the ventilation of feelings, self-detachment and a range of problem-focused strategies.

As a rule of thumb in dealing with stress, it is usually helpful to start with the most straightforward approach, and if you can accept the reality of a situation then you have already put yourself in the best position to resolve it. *Acceptance* is a functional coping response where the source of stress cannot easily be changed and you are able to recognise that it will need to be accommodated in some way. The general message, here, is that you should not attempt to control the uncontrollable – if a stressor cannot be changed you can retain a sense of control by changing your expectations and attitudes, looking for the positive side of a situation and accepting that the world is rarely perfect and that people make mistakes. Job satisfaction also tends to be enhanced when your work-related thinking combines both optimistic and pessimistic perceptions into *balanced expectations*. Positive or engaged coping mechanisms often have their roots in finding a balance between a hopeful interpretation of the situation and a realistic appreciation of its difficulties or stressors, with awareness of the possibilities for progress or change co-existing alongside an acknowledgement of the constraints.

You can also apply techniques with which you will already be familiar from the field of cognitive behavioural therapy (CBT). For example, *positive reappraisal* is a type of emotion-focused coping aimed at managing distress. Talking about emotions and feelings can help to put stressful circumstances into a broader or wider perspective, so that you see them in a more favourable light. This might involve making a positive social comparison with others in a worse position, reappraising a situation as one which could happen to anyone or using humour appropriately. 'Stress inoculation' is another CBT approach that you can use to cope when you are feeling stressed. By consciously giving yourself time to plan, you can prepare yourself for a difficult or challenging situation, *rehearsing* a number of possible responses in advance, for example in a learning set or supervision session.

In the early stages of dealing with a stressful situation, it may also be helpful to seek opportunities to *ventilate your feelings*, avoiding catastrophising demanding events by expressing your feelings, rather than letting them build up inside. Failing to voice feelings, in an open, honest and respectful manner, often means that the situation has no chance to improve and is more likely to deteriorate. However, this approach is probably best employed on a restricted basis, as overuse for prolonged periods can impede adjustment, distracting you from active coping and moving on to more positive reappraisal. Increased levels of *self-detachment* have also been shown to protect against emotional exhaustion in social work (Ying 2008). This type of coping is fostered by making efforts to stand back from your experiences, so that you are protected against an overidentification with subjective emotions. It also involves recognising that what you perceive as your own shortcomings or difficulties are often part of the wider human condition, experienced by almost everyone at some time in their lives, and that you therefore need to employ a measure of forgiveness in relation to your own shortcomings, rather than harsh, critical judgement and self-blame.

Positive *problem-focused strategies*, involving active engagement in thinking about how to cope with a stressor – gathering information and coming up with what practical steps to take – can also be employed. Even in apparently uncontrollable or deteriorating situations, it is possible to identify goals, and experience efficacy, mastery and control in working towards them. Problem-focused coping helps to focus your attention, and has clear parallels with your existing knowledge, skills and understanding of task-centred practice. By approaching a difficulty or stressor in this way, you will be nurturing positive feelings of your effectiveness and control, both of which have been shown to be critical elements in maintaining positive well-being (Collins 2007). This type of coping is fostered by identifying your priorities, putting other activities aside in order to focus without distraction on a particular stressor, consciously putting time and space between yourself and a stressor to avoid acting prematurely, setting standards that are reasonable and learning to be content with some things that are 'good enough'. Trying to be perfect is a major source of avoidable stress; and taking time to reflect on the positive things in your life, including your personal abilities, talents and interests away from work, is likely to be beneficial.

Finally, returning to the exercise that has run throughout the chapter (see Box 10.3), there is an opportunity now to reflect on your own coping mechanisms, and how you might work more effectively with stressful situations in the future.

Box 10.3 How do you work with stressful situations?
PART 3: COPING MECHANISMS
Reflect further on the work situation that you identified for this exercise at the beginning of the chapter.

- What was the outcome of your coping response?

- How satisfied were you with it?

- Are there any alternative coping strategies that could help you improve your responses and the outcome in a similar situation in future?

Key considerations in dealing with stress, emotion and exhaustion

- Stress *can* be good for you. Some degree of stress can be a positive, motivational incentive to achieve things that you might not have thought possible. Stress only becomes harmful when there is a loss of balance between what is being demanded of you and the resources available to you to meet those demands.

- Balance is an important theme in dealing with stress. Positive coping is rooted in finding a balance between a hopeful interpretation of a situation and a realistic appraisal of its difficulties or constraints.

- Demands, constraints and personal characteristics are the three key elements affecting workplace stress and job satisfaction. Identifying the interactions between critical factors particular to your own situation, within these three domains, might provide you with an early warning of any imbalances that are developing, and trigger a timely look at your coping strategies.

• Helpful strategies to be nurtured and fostered are those that are either problem-focused, aimed at reducing or removing entirely whatever has caused the stress, or emotion-focused, where the cause of the stress lies outside your control and reducing the distress is your main aim.

• Trying to control the uncontrollable will put you in an impossible position. Recognising and separating out what you can affect from that which is beyond your control will make a really positive contribution to your psychological well-being.

Chapter 11

Working in a Satisfying Climate

- Understanding the organisation
- Becoming an effective organisational operator
- Key considerations for working in a satisfying climate

Much of this chapter is concerned with strategies, structures and cultures over which you may feel, particularly as a new member of staff, you have little power and influence. However, developing a better understanding of how your own position, practice and role fit within an overall corporate plan should enhance your ability to become an effective professional. By maintaining an active stance, in which you understand and take responsibility for your own role, you are also likely to become a more satisfied member of the team.

Understanding the organisation

There are three primary aspects of the organisation which will have an impact on how you experience your place within it and the quality of your working life. Broadly, these are its structure and strategies, culture, and climate. None of these elements is static, and each has a dynamic interrelation with the others, in constant flux as different imperatives, political and personal, financial and strategic, wax and wane. You might think of this 'organisational triangle' as similar to the Bermuda Triangle, in which people, rather than ships, can disappear unless certain precautions are taken.

Structure and strategy

We have already referred in Chapter 5 to the importance of obtaining an organisational structure diagram as part of your induction programme, to help you visualise your place within the corporate picture. Without a clear understanding about the roles and responsibilities of different staff within the organisation, confused or conflicting messages can arise which exacerbate feelings of division between frontline workers and their line managers, and a 'them and us' culture can take root.

The physical environment also plays an important part in shaping your relationship with work. For example, where the office building is situated in the community, how accessible it is and what security measures are in place may all be important factors affecting your day-to-day comings and goings. Inside, the increasing trend towards open-plan office accommodation has advantages, in that the closeness of team members can be supportive, but there can also be disadvantages, for example if there is limited privacy, or it is difficult to find a quiet space in which to complete written work, or you feel that you are under constant scrutiny. Hot desking is another policy increasingly prevalent in health and local authority settings, which can severely reduce opportunities to build supportive relationships with colleagues and, importantly, to have regular contact with other social workers. Home working may sometimes be appropriate, but on a regular basis it can increase your isolation from the organisation, peers and colleagues.

At the head of the most common hierarchical, bureaucratic agency structure, strategic managers have been called the 'social architects' of the organisation, responsible for designing its purposes, vision and values. The vision – where we are going, and the strategies – how we will get there – will be passed down to be enacted by those in the tiers below. Not infrequently, there is a significant gap between what strategic managers say in a mission statement and what is actually carried out in the organisation. First line managers occupy a pivotal position in a hierarchical structure because they have key responsibilities in two directions, which can sometimes operate in opposition to one another.

> I suppose the most difficult thing is managing time and managing competing demands from below and above really.

> You are very much in the middle of the sandwich I think as a
> first line manager. (Line manager)

They are charged with implementing the policies and strategies handed down to them from the higher tiers, and for directing the day-to-day work, while also fostering positive attitudes and beliefs in the organisational mission among the staff whom they supervise and support in the delivery of services. The ways in which your manager is able to deal with these tensions will certainly influence your opinion of their organisational effectiveness. There is more on leadership and being led in Chapter 12.

Often promoted from a professional practice background, first line managers frequently find that they lack some of the leadership and management skills, related to the specific task of managing a team of social workers, as the following managers from our research mentioned:

> I think it was after about 9 months that I was sent on some
> training – about supervision – so that was nice – you do it first
> and then get taught how to do it. I don't think there's a very
> good programme really for managers.

> The training courses that are set up often don't meet the need
> because they're too late and they're not directed specifically
> at what you're doing. (First line managers in local authority
> teams)

Although not specifically concerned with social work, Harrison (1972), looking at the character of organisations in general, grouped them into four broad types according to their primary drivers and orientation, as set out in Table 11.1.

Table 11.1 Organisational orientation

Organisation type	Characteristics
Power-oriented	• attempts to dominate the internal and external environment • managed through absolute control over subordinates • little attention to human values and welfare • competitive • driven by struggle for personal advantage
Role-oriented	• bureaucratic • emphasis on legality, legitimacy and responsibility • conflict regulated by rules and procedures • rights and privileges defined and adhered to • emphasis on hierarchy and status • predictable, stable and respectable
Task-oriented	• structures, functions and activities all focused on organisational goals • dominated by task accomplishment • individuals trained to perform task competently or replaced • authority derived from appropriate knowledge and competence • rapid and flexible organisation • collaboration to promote goal achievement
People-oriented	• exists to serve the needs of the members • authority only occasionally assigned by task competence • influence through individual example and helpfulness • decision-making using consensus methods • roles assigned by personal preference • focus on individual need for learning and growth

Source: adapted from Harrison (1972)

The organisation in which you work probably doesn't fall into any one category completely, but some of its characteristics will no doubt be recognisable. Since an increasing amount of work undertaken by social workers occurs within a statutory framework, social workers are likely to find themselves working in organisations which are bureaucratic, and while these have traditionally fitted best into Harrison's role-oriented category, the focus in much professional development on competence, and the emphasis in all public services on performance indicators and outputs, may well place organisations employing social workers closer to the task-oriented category. For example, in a task-oriented organisation, collaboration is a characteristic used to promote goal achievement, and certainly multi-agency working and greater coordination of services are now a central tenet of government policy for public services right across the UK.

In any form of social work practice, the influence of the wider environment in which service users are living is always a focus of attention, and it may be useful to remember that organisations are themselves situated within communities, with the reputation and local standing of the agency likely to have an impact on how you feel and indeed how you are perceived by others – service users and professionals. This was well illustrated by an experienced care manager taking part in a pilot project with carers in GP surgeries, evaluated by one of the authors. The care manager was seconded to the GP surgery from the local social services office for one day each week. In her substantive post with social services, she was used to being greeted on the telephone with a certain ambivalence or lack of interest in her offers of help, and she was shocked to find that by simply announcing herself as coming from the GP surgery, she could 'feel people standing to attention' at the other end of the telephone. She also reported a real temptation to adopt a different telephone voice for her surgery 'persona'.

Culture

Culture can be thought of as the 'social glue' of the organisation. As well as being influenced by structures and strategies, the environment in which you work will also depend on 'shared ways of seeing, thinking and doing' which can be termed collectively as the organisational culture, variously expressed as follows:

- how things get done around here

- values and expectations which organisation members come to share

- the social glue that holds the organisation together

- the taken for granted and shared meanings that people assign to their social surroundings.

(Hawkins and Shohet 2006, p.168)

Depending on your standpoint, culture can be viewed as something that an organisation 'has', which can be changed or imposed by management, or it can be seen as what the organisation 'is', a summation of the ideas, beliefs and values of those who make up the organisation (Thompson *et al.* 1996). Whichever is the dominant approach will have a profound effect on your experience of working in a particular agency.

Lysons (1997) likened culture to an iceberg, which we have represented in the form of a triangle in Figure 11.1.

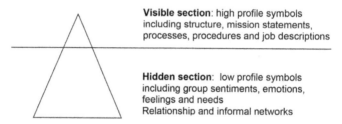

Figure 11.1 Visible and hidden aspects of organisational culture

The diagram shows that what is most noticeable about culture is the high profile symbols, designed to communicate ideas and assumptions to the external as well as the internal world through such things as prestige buildings or events, logos and mission statements. However, of more significance to those *inside* the organisation are the low profile symbols, such as the day-to-day practice experiences of workers and service users, the use of particular language or jargon, how meetings are called and by whom, and the ways in which decisions are made, communicated and implemented. In many instances, there can be a dissonance between the high and low profile symbols. For example, an organisation may have an impressive policy about the key importance of ongoing professional development, yet fail to provide the backfill and release arrangements that translate that policy into a practical reality for frontline staff, as the following NQSW noted.

> Yes, most definitely. The agency are committed to it [post-qualifying training] yes, they can do the financial bit, but in terms of all the other things – mentoring, support, release and backfill – well, it's just not there. (NQSW)

Organisations are composed of people, and organisational behaviours, attitudes and values are therefore dependent, to a large extent, on the beliefs held by individual members. A healthy culture depends on how well individual beliefs and motivations are aligned with those of the organisation. Again, this interrelationship will not be a static one, and Figure 11.2 uses the iceberg analogy again to represent stages in breakdown, if the organisational culture loses its integrity and becomes fractured. Which of the diagrams best portrays the current position of your organisation, do you think?

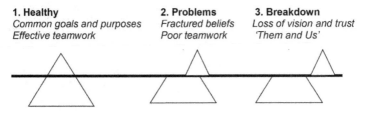

1. Healthy
Common goals and purposes
Effective teamwork

2. Problems
Fractured beliefs
Poor teamwork

3. Breakdown
Loss of vision and trust
'Them and Us'

Figure 11.2 Aligned and fractured cultures (adapted from Thody *et al.* 2007)

Organisations frequently attempt to deal with the potential for fracture in this way by introducing an overarching philosophy, defining a common purpose, goals and priorities, but the success of this approach will ultimately depend on the ownership of the philosophy by all groups employed within the organisation. Organisational culture cannot simply be imposed from above, but must also involve consultation and participation, making it relevant to the work at each level within the organisation. This brings us back to an understanding of culture as something that is part of the organisation's *being* rather than something handed down from above.

So far we have discussed culture as if it applies in a homogeneous way across the whole organisation, whereas in reality culture is often complex and multilayered. For example, different departments or teams within the same organisation may develop a variation or subculture within the corporate whole. These subcultures can have a beneficial effect if they increase a sense of common ownership and purpose within a team, but equally they may result in conflict and tensions. There are a number of dysfunctional cultural dynamics that can all too commonly come to dominate the 'way things are done around here', and each of those identified by Hawkins and Shohet (2006) is worth a brief mention:

BLAME

This type of culture is rooted in seeking out and blaming individual failings for what are, in truth, organisational difficulties. Managers with this mindset deny or marginalise the significance of the organisation's contribution to any dysfunction, stress or conflict, preferring to identify a difficult or problematic person, who, if they cannot be brought into line, might need to be removed. Scapegoating like this can happen at every level in an organisation, and even within a team, in the belief that efficiency can be regained if only the problematic person can be 'sorted out'. The real danger of accepting this type of culture is that, in attempting to avoid being identified as the problem person, you end up denying your own needs for support and become stifled by secrecy, attempting to struggle on alone.

BUREAUCRATIC EFFICIENCY

Bureaucracy frequently comes to dominate an organisational culture, perhaps as a defence against anxiety in the context of the complexity and uncertainty which characterise much social work practice. This can be a particular problem, for example, in safeguarding work with children and families, or in the assessment and management of mental capacity, both of which involve high levels of uncertainty and risk. In these circumstances, safe and effective performance is necessarily guided by rules about who is authorised to make certain decisions, and it is also appropriate to have processes aimed at ensuring that no one person is left in isolation, holding sole responsibility for difficult decisions. While there is much in the bureaucratic approach that is therefore potentially helpful, you need to be aware of its potential limitations as well. For example, assessment systems used to identify needs and match them to resources can reduce complex issues to oversimplistic categories, narrowing your professional autonomy and any chance of a creative response to service users' problems.

COMPETITION

Although it is at odds with many of the core values of social work, competition is a common feature of working within many organisations these days. Not only is the organisation itself likely to be engaging in competition with others for resources, but there will also be groups, subgroups, rivalries and personality clashes in the pursuit of resources, power and influence *within* the organisation. Hierarchical organisations, like those found throughout the NHS, are particularly prone to a culture of competition, which can also take on greater significance for staff in organisations that are undergoing change and reorganisation, with the attendant threat of redeployment or redundancy.

CRISIS

An organisation driven by crisis can be recognised by the lack of priority given to the creation and maintenance of uninterrupted time for reflection and forward planning. Practice in this culture is dominated by 'the moment', in which ad hoc responses and decision-making in a hurry, before the next deluge, predominate. Where this type of culture prevails, service users soon learn that the best way to get attention is to precipitate a crisis, thus establishing a self-perpetuating cycle.

ADDICTION

Finally, there is an organisational culture which can be viewed through the metaphor of addiction. It is possible for the organisation itself to behave like an addictive substance, producing workaholism in particular individuals, who forsake any sustainable work/life balance as their 'addiction' overtakes them. Faced with an addicted member, others within the team or management tier either collude or develop a codependency. Although mostly covert, this culture delivers the message that to forego breaks and to work late is 'the way things are done around here'.

Climate

Structure and culture combine to create what can be thought of as the 'climate', which is essentially a reflection of the way that staff *feel* about the organisation for which they are working. The organisational climate can have a profound influence on the way in which you engage with the world of work. In a satisfying climate, you will feel able to work with energy and commitment, while dissatisfaction can lead, over time, to distancing and depersonalisation. For each member of staff, the way that they interpret the organisational climate in which they are working depends, to a large extent, on the degree of congruence between how they want to practise and their perception of what is needed or demanded of them by their employing agency. You may already be aware of the extent to which any areas of mismatch can influence your attitude to work.

Importantly, organisational climate has been shown to be a significant predictor of both the quality and outcomes of services for children, with improvements in psychosocial functioning significantly greater for children serviced by offices with more positive climates (Glisson and Hemmelgarn 1998). Their study looked at several aspects of the workplace to assess the quality of the organisational climate, and you might find it interesting to consider the statements in Box 11.1 (page 210) in relation to your own workplace.

How far do the areas of strong disagreement, where you have scored 4 or 5, represent areas of mismatch between the requirements of the job and personal principle? It is possible to become caught up in the organisation's own conflicting values, which often reflect a discrepancy between the lofty mission statement and the daily experience of work.

Box 11.1 Assessing the organisational climate

What sort of climate are you currently working in?

Record your response to each of the statements below by ticking one box in each row and adding up the total scores.

	Strongly agree 1	2	3	4	5 Strongly disagree
My agency treats me fairly	o	o	o	o	o
My role is clearly defined	o	o	o	o	o
I have sufficient time to complete my tasks each day	o	o	o	o	o
I balance care and control well within my role	o	o	o	o	o
Cooperation with other agencies is good	o	o	o	o	o
My professional development is encouraged	o	o	o	o	o
Job satisfaction here is high	o	o	o	o	o
Emotional exhaustion is low	o	o	o	o	o
I experience high levels of personal accomplishment	o	o	o	o	o
Practice is always client centred	o	o	o	o	o
Totals	□	□	□	□	□

A low score overall (< 30) indicates an organisation which provides a positive climate for staff; higher scores (> 31) indicate a more negative climate.

What steps could you take, individually, or along with your supervisor, manager or team, to improve the areas of strong disagreement or person/job mismatch?

Becoming an effective organisational operator
Managing conflict

Social work can be a stressful job, and some of that stress will inevitably be caused by conflict, not only with service users but also with colleagues, supervisors and managers. Recognising that conflict is a normal part of everyday life is a helpful starting point, and the experience need not be entirely negative. Positive outcomes, such as improved relationships and personal development, can emerge if conflicts are acknowledged and successfully resolved, although inappropriate responses, such as violence and aggression, must never be tolerated. In these extreme circumstances, you should turn to the agency's safety policy if the difficulties are with service users, or to the harassment and bullying at work policies if you are experiencing problems with colleagues or managers.

Since it is largely unavoidable, the important issue is how you respond to conflict when it does arise. Five styles of response are commonly identified from research (Hughes and Wearing 2007, p.105):

- *integrating*: a collaborative style that seeks to maximise advantages for both parties

- *compromising*: both parties give some ground to resolve the issue

- *obliging*: one person denies their own interests by acceding to the other's position

- *avoiding*: one party withdraws from the conflict and consequently the other's position prevails

- *forcing*: one party forces their interests to be accepted at the expense of the other's.

You may have experienced one or all of these styles of response to conflict at different times in your working life, but an integrating style would appear to fit most comfortably with social work values and to have the greatest chance of success in reducing disruption in the workplace. It is also noticeable that the three principal formal processes for conflict resolution, namely negotiation, mediation and arbitration, all incorporate an integrating style, to a greater or lesser extent. The particular value of negotiation is that, by paying attention to both the substance of the disagreement and the relationship of the parties involved, resolution can be achieved in such a way that neither party feels that they are the losers.

Negotiation is based on four principles (Lens 2004):

1. *Separate the person from the problem*: Hold back from blame in order to create a positive working relationship, recognising that emotions and hurt feelings can become part of the equation.

2. *Focus on interests not positions*: Take a step back to look for any common interests, as a focus for consideration, through which the parties can be brought together in active and more purposeful dialogue.

3. *Consider options for mutual gain*: View the situation from a number of perspectives and look for different solutions, each with the other party's interests in mind.

4. *Use objective criteria*: Try to define some criteria as headings under which to consider options, actions and outcomes. Procedural fairness is important, and identifying agreed criteria in the process can help to ensure that decisions are based not on a battle of wills, but on an evaluation of 'best fit', given the particular circumstances.

As a general rule, it is always best to try to resolve disagreements directly with those concerned through informal discussion, at the earliest opportunity and the lowest possible level within the organisational hierarchy.

Assessing teamwork

Social workers most often work in teams, and in Chapter 8 we looked at teams from the point of view of support, considering some of the roles and stages in their formation.

Box 11.2 Assessing effective teamwork

Think of a team of which you are a part. Using a scale of 1–10, where 1 is low and 10 is high, score each statement to reflect your opinion of the quality of the teamwork of which you are a part.

		Score
Purpose and direction	We have a sense of purpose	
	We know where we are going	
Communication	We communicate well within the team	
	We know what is going on in other teams	
Decision-making	We make clear, timely decisions	
	We act on decisions when agreed	
Participation	I am involved in policy/organisation issues	
	I am supported and monitored in my work	
Openness and trust	I feel comfortable to speak openly	
	We can disagree without difficulty	
Use of time	We use our time together well	
	We focus on important issues	
Tasks	We share tasks fairly	
	Tasks are allocated to match interests and abilities	

Source: adapted from Thody *et al.* (2007)

Now that you have had some time to observe its workings at close quarters, it might be opportune to review some of the characteristics of your own team, making an assessment of its effectiveness, and your own contribution to the quality of teamwork, by completing the questionnaire about effective teamwork in Box 11.2.

Most social workers place great value on their teams and feel supported by them, but that is not to say that defensive or negative attitudes may not develop from time to time, and in these circumstances it is important to try to understand why individuals are feeling as they do. Most commonly, successful teamwork is thwarted by a range of organisational barriers. For instance, if a group is larger than six to eight people, fully collaborative work is less easy, and it might be a good idea to delegate a smaller subgroup to undertake a specific task on behalf of the larger body of people. Work overload, resulting in tasks not being completed, little time for review and unfair allocation of responsibilities may also undermine teamwork, as can a lack of leadership or organisational change, both of which can result in a lack of purpose and participation, as well as poor decision-making. Management texts and handbooks abound in which it is acknowledged, as a general truth, that the key to a successful organisation is effective teamwork. However, the complexities of working in a team should never be underestimated. Skills in teamwork are rarely part of professional training or induction, and are something that you are more likely to be expected to pick up as you go along, almost by osmosis, as you might learn the skills of being a parent.

According to Belbin (2004), a 'super team', composed entirely of clever people, does not guarantee effectiveness. He has shown that critical thinkers tended to be 'critical' in both senses of the word, and, when faced with a problem, thus found a large number of more negative things to say which preoccupied their time in endless thinking and debate, while also alienating other members of the team socially, and interfering with the integration and general cohesion of the group. Although proposing and opposing are important processes in team decision-making, there are other equally important aspects which cannot be neglected if the team is to be an effective one. Gathering resources, collecting and organising information, recording current knowledge and coordinating plans and action are all equally important activities. All of this points to the necessity for a broad skills mix within teams, and completing the questionnaire in Box 11.2 (page 213) might help you to assess the quality of the teamwork in which you are involved. If team members have sufficient courage, it might be informative for a whole group to complete the exercise and discuss their assessments with one another.

Accountability

Being held individually accountable for their work is one of the key differences identified by NQSWs as they move from student to employee, and this individual accountability is responsible for much of the '*thud!*' associated with acquiring professional status discussed in Part I. Corbett's (1991) framework includes four broad dimensions of organisational accountability, as illustrated in Figure 11.3.

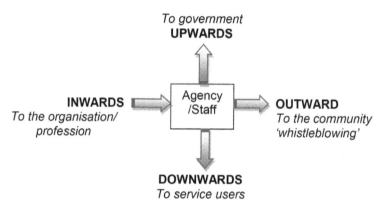

Figure 11.3 Organisational accountabilities

Accountability for social workers is multiplied by the number of different 'constituencies' which hold social work to account, of which Banks (2002) identifies four forms:

- *technical accountability*: related to knowledge about what works and skills in how to do things

- *procedural accountability*: set out in regulations, guidance and agency procedures

- *managerial accountability*: in response to orders or requests from organisational managers, and

- *ethical accountability*: based on values, codes of conduct and personal understandings of what is right and wrong.

Deciding how to combine and manage these different forms of accountability understandably presents a confusing picture for NQSWs, but the codes of practice developed by each of the four

UK care councils provide clear guidance, and the procedures for registration of title and regular re-registration now ensure the maintenance of professionally accountable standards.

Performance measurement is closely linked to accountability, but difficulties arise if 'outcomes' turn out to be process measures that emphasise the quantity of what was produced over any consideration of its quality. It has been shown that improved 'outputs', such as availability, responsiveness, and information-sharing, do not necessarily equate to improved outcomes for service users (e.g. Glisson and Hemmelgar 1998; Scottish Executive 2002). Although these matters are likely to be of greater concern to your manager in relation to the service overall, monitoring the quality of your own performance, and keeping a record in your professional development file, as part of your professional development plan, can also be a worthwhile activity, incorporating feedback from service users, carers, other professionals and agencies, to develop your understanding of what is key in defining the quality of what you are providing.

Key considerations for working in a satisfying climate

Drawing on the work of Charles and Butler (2004), you might find the following checklist helpful in identifying a number of practical ways in which you can contribute to the development of a satisfying organisational climate:

- Build professional credibility by attending to self-image. Professional credibility is established by very simple actions, such as being organised, punctual, having an uncluttered desk and producing concise and timely reports. If you are regarded as someone whose organisational abilities and time-management skills are exemplary, you may find other people have a greater willingness to listen to you when you need to say no to additional work or inappropriate tasks.

- Take control of your professional development. Think about linking your preferences for development to any 'skill shortages' or specific niches in the team/group/agency, developing yourself as a resource on which colleagues can rely.

- Accept that hierarchical organisations are frequently limited in the ways in which they work with emotion. In these circumstances it is vital to use personnel procedures to look after yourself, for example planning and taking your full leave entitlement, taking time off in lieu when you have worked additional hours and taking sick leave when appropriate.

- Avoid conspiracy theory as a way of understanding agency decision-making, and accept contradictions as a reflection of organisational complexity (for example, when some of the intentions set out in a mission statement are not delivered in practice).

- Taking a self-critical, flexible and adaptive stance will maximise your capacity, albeit at the micro-level, to influence organisational change.

Chapter 12

Managing Increasing Complexity

- Building on critical reflection
- Leadership and being led
- The learning organisation
- Key considerations for managing increasing complexity

In this final chapter we explore some of the links between critical reflection, reflective practice and 'learning organisations', as you develop your professional identity and take on increasingly complex work. Gould and Baldwin (2004) have linked reflective learning with learning organisations through a discussion of three models of problem-solving. First, as presented in Chapter 2, we know that professionals draw on formal knowledge and research to guide their interventions, but their strategies for problem-solving are derived from a set of individual, situational rules developed from experience in the workplace over time. Second, practice which is generally understood as applied formal knowledge pays insufficient attention to the influence that context has on how knowledge is put to use. Despite widespread references to skill transfer as a core competence in social work, there is evidence to show that practical knowledge is actually very context-specific, so the successful transfer of learning cannot take place without some reworking and adaptation. Third, 'the problem' itself is a matter of interpretation depending on the context, in contrast to 'rule-based' approaches to practice where there is an assumption that there are problem types to which predetermined solutions can then be applied.

These core premises of the development of professional practice have strong synergy with those of learning organisations, in which learning is understood to be ongoing and embedded in the organisational context. In other words, learning is not confined to attending a course or undertaking formal training, but also occurs in the workplace, often in informal and unplanned ways, and on a continuing basis.

Building on critical reflection
Decision-making and uncertainty

In Chapters 2 and 3 we considered the development of professional expertise through the transformation of context-free rules into your own repertoire of situational rules, applied to an increasing range of practice situations and informed by overarching and underpinning knowledge intertwined in increasingly complex and creative ways. Decision-making or professional judgement can therefore be seen as calling for an active synthesis of the components at the corners of the triangle in Figure 12.1, while also responding to the uniqueness, complexity and uncertainty of each individual situation. Managing these dynamic tensions draws on many of your graduate skills, and is the antithesis of the application of the rigid mechanistic procedures associated with managerialism.

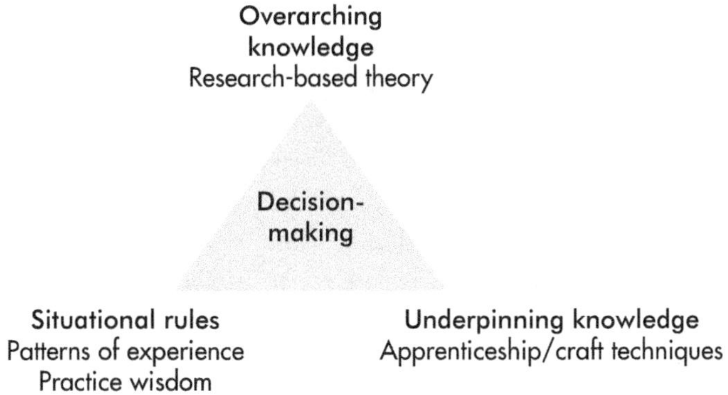

Overarching
knowledge
Research-based theory

Decision-
making

Situational rules   Underpinning knowledge
Patterns of experience   Apprenticeship/craft techniques
Practice wisdom

Figure 12.1 Developing judgement and decision-making

Decision-making in social work is generally understood to follow a rational approach, assuming that people act in a logical, linear way, choosing options that bring the highest returns for the least costs. This focus on rational choices fits well with evidence-based approaches to practice, based as they are on the quasi-scientific selection and evaluation of different courses of action. Within this framework, the decision-making process can be divided into a number of stages in which the problem is defined, alternatives generated and selected according to available information, and action implemented, followed up by the monitoring and evaluation of the results. The whole process becomes a repeating cycle, with new problems defined according to the evaluation of the outcomes of previous decisions.

However, this description represents a rather idealised version of how decisions are reached in practice. As the following response from a social worker in our own research suggests, the everyday experience of decision-making for most social workers is more likely to be messier and more unpredictable than that outlined above, constrained by factors such as a lack of information, the degree of complexity of the problems faced, the limited capacity of individuals to process information, the short timeframes within which a decision is required, and conflict between different goals.

> I can honestly say, since qualifying...I haven't looked at a single paper, a single piece of research. In the field, well it's very limited...you don't have the range of journals available to you...and more importantly, its time. (Social worker – 6 months post-qualification)

What is needed in these circumstances is the capacity to live with and to tolerate a significant degree of ambiguity and even paradox. The world does not divide easily into what's unambiguously good for service users and what's not, what's safe and what isn't. The truth is often that we don't know, and that it really does 'all depend'. In *War and Peace*, Tolstoy included some wonderful descriptions about how battles, which look very clear to historians with the benefit of hindsight, never actually seem that way to those involved at the time. These passages were meant as a metaphor for society, to show that there is seldom a vantage point from which it is possible to get the full picture, in the here and now.

French (2001) quotes Keats, who coined the term 'negative capability' to describe a state in which a person is 'capable of being in uncertainties, mysteries, doubts, without any irritable reaching after fact and reason'. His negative capability is the ability to stick with the sometimes frightening fact that, in certain situations, we simply do not know. Where negative capability fails, your energies become 'dispersed' in one of three ways, through explanation, emotional reaction or physical action. These reactions may be very familiar to you, either as part of your own responses to complex and uncertain situations, or as behaviours that you have seen in others, at work or elsewhere. Negative capability describes the capacity to tolerate the emotional impact of the uncertainties and doubts that professional life can throw at you. Developing negative capability means that you are able to stay with the moment, to wait, holding tensions and anxieties, living with problems that may be intractable, accepting paradoxes and dilemmas for what they are, conserving and preserving your energies to discover a new thought, idea or possibility for more meaningful, positive action (French 2001).

Reflection in and on action

Part of this vital ability to 'stay with the moment' is developed and strengthened through the practice of reflection. As a student social worker, you will have been required to produce written reflections on your practice to demonstrate that you were developing the insight and awareness needed to become a qualified social worker.

Box 12.1 Framework for reflection on action

Answer the following questions in relation to a recent example from your practice.

- Description
    - Describe the situation, identifying the important issues and participants
- Reflection
    - What were you trying to do?
    - Why did you take the actions that you did?

- What were the consequences for each participant?
- How did you feel? How did others feel?
- What did they do or say to let you know how they felt?
- How did you show how you were feeling?

- Influencing factors
  - What internal and external factors influenced your decisions?
  - What knowledge and skills did or should have influenced you?
  - What should not have influenced you?

- Alternatives
  - What could you have been done differently?
  - What other choices could you have made?
  - What would have been the consequences of those choices?

- Learning
  - How can you make sense of this experience, considering both the past and what you could do in the future?
  - How do you feel now?
  - Have you taken action to support yourself and others as a result of this experience?
  - How have you changed?
  - Have others changed?
  - Is there anything more you need to do as a result? For instance, search out information, undertake some training or reading, etc.

Source: adapted from Johns (1994)

As a qualified professional, however, reflection is no longer about evidence for others, but rather a means by which you choose to develop your practice for yourself, so that you are comfortable and secure in the ideas and approaches that inform your own decision-making.

Reflection can be broken down into two separate, but linked, components. Reflection on action is focused on thinking about what you have already done, in order to inform what you will do in the future. Box 12.1 on the previous page provides a framework for thinking about this type of reflection.

However, reflection is not a process that takes place only after the fact. It also occurs, consciously or not, at the time of the event in question – referred to as reflection in action. This type of reflection requires that you, metaphorically, take a step back from what you are doing at the time that you are doing it, disengaging from the 'automatic' part of what you are doing and thinking critically about your practice, to make sure that you have paid appropriate attention to every aspect, even as you are actively engaged in the process. Taking these ideas a little further, Barnett (1997) has identified three overlapping domains of critical practice (as shown in Figure 12.2).

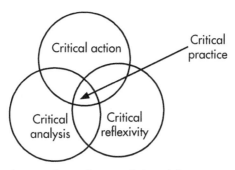

Figure 12.2 The domains of critical practice (adapted from Barnett 1997)

- *Critical analysis* involves the evaluation of knowledge, theories, policies and practice from multiple perspectives, as part of a commitment to ongoing enquiry as you analyse the situation.

- *Critical action* calls for a repertoire of skills, taking account of the context of each situation, working with difference and recognising and challenging power inequalities and structural disadvantage.

- *Critical reflexivity* is about maintaining an aware, reflective and engaged self, questioning personal assumptions and values.

Critical reflexivity in particular is a key ingredient in establishing the interactive and circular processes which underpin critical practice, requiring a highly developed sense of self-awareness. The better you know yourself, the more able and open you become to new learning, while adapting and developing flexible and creative approaches to practice, its problems and decision-making dilemmas.

According to Fook and Gardener (2007, p.51), the broad purpose of critical reflection is to 'unsettle the fundamental or dominant thinking implicit in professional practices, in order to see other ways of practising'. It is about unearthing and examining anew your own daily assumptions, including those that may have become lost or obfuscated by internal agency directives. Critical reflection is about finding better ways to practise (action) based on different ways of thinking (analysis). It is the ability to link both aspects of action and analysis that is important.

> But the people who read the papers hate social workers... so in the end you realise that we're a powerless, oppressed, disadvantaged group of individuals which is quite sad really because you're looking at some superb people. I've never worked with people who care so much and have so many skills. (NQSW)

Practitioners, like the one above, often report feeling powerless and lacking in professional autonomy, but taking an active stance and making use of critical reflection, both in and on action, can produce a number of real benefits for your practice.

Leadership and being led

As well as consciously using reflection on and in action to deal with the increasingly complex work that you will be expected to take on as you develop as a professional, the way that colleagues and others do their jobs, particularly those in positions of power within the organisation, such as team leaders and managers, will also play an important role in your practice.

Leadership and management are almost interchangeable expressions in everyday terms, and certainly there are a number of attributes and skills common to both roles. Management meets the day-to-day requirements for most teams operating in a stable environment, but when conditions become more complex, unpredictable or subject to rapid change, rather more is needed by way of leadership which is creative and focuses on helping the team to cope and continue to function effectively.

Good leadership and management are central to the development of a healthy organisational culture, and although we, perhaps, no longer believe in the concept of the born leader, imbued with heroic qualities, there will be certain key attributes that you use to assess the quality of your leaders or managers, which might include:

- empathy and understanding

- consistency and fairness

- acceptance and respect

- integrity and honesty, and

- reliability and trustworthiness.

None of these attributes on its own is enough to characterise an outstanding leader, but to deliver the full set, consistently and coherently, to a range of different people, certainly requires skills which will take time to develop (see Box 12.2, page 226). However, this does not mean that some of the foundations for good leadership skills cannot be laid down at the very beginning of your career. In fact, the sooner you start the better. You can begin to develop your own leadership skills by:

- communicating effectively and honestly

- fostering good relationships with others both inside and outside your employing organisation

- focusing on your own personal and professional development

- developing your critical thinking skills and evidence-based practice, so that you are in a position to offer information, advice and support to others, and

- helping others with problem-solving, planning and getting things done.

Box 12.2 Appraising management skills
Think of the best manager you have ever had.

- How did that person make you feel?
- What skills did that person possess?
- How did they use their skills?

Skills for Care has produced a social work leadership toolkit which includes a range of manager induction standards (SfC 2013) in England. These specify what managers and leaders need to do, including the following list, which appears in the core and optional standards:

- governance and accountability
- systems and processes to promote communication
- partnership working and relationships
- using person-centred practice to achieve positive outcomes
- team leadership and management
- managing resources
- equality, diversity and inclusion
- safeguarding and protection
- professional development
- change and growth
- managing business
- ensuring quality.

Two main themes can be identified from this list – a concern for *people* and a concern for *task*. Achieving a balance between these two aspects is a primary focus for managers, both in the day-to-day running of a team, and in some of the more specific aspects of their role, such as supervision. Different permutations of these two domains can be linked to the four leadership styles summarised in Table 12.1, each of which may already be familiar to you.

Table 12.1 Leadership styles

Leadership style	Benefits	Disadvantages
Social Concern for people No concern for task	Interpersonal skills flourish Good communication Team feels valued	Lack of direction for team Things appear disorganised Not much progresses
Authoritarian Concern for task No concern for people	Vision delivered with clarity Well-defined rules, schedules Tasks accomplished	No credit for creativity, difference No room for individual input Blame can become widespread
Impoverished No concern for people No concern for task	Minimum interference Team members are free to do what they like	No support Followers feel 'rudderless'
Team Concern for people Concern for task	Team highly motivated and valued Tasks accomplished	Can give rise to over-reliance on one individual and personal charisma

The four categories of leadership describe theoretical styles, and provide rather artificial boundaries. If you had to choose one, a leader with a team style, showing concern for people *and* for task might be your preferred option. However, in the real world, a successful leader might need to draw on a mix of strategies, according to the circumstances. Sometimes task-achievement must be prioritised, so a more authoritarian approach may be needed, but there will also be times, for example when the team needs to relax, when a more social style will be appropriate. As in much else in life, the key to success lies not in a table of prescribed options, but in the ability to understand the team and its context, and to assess what is necessary to encourage best practice and professional development.

You will also expect a good leader to stand behind the team and support it, as well as getting outside constituencies to support the team's efforts. Leaders need to be able to 'read' and understand others in the workplace, and to use this knowledge to influence them positively to enhance personal as well as organisational objectives. Ahearn and colleagues (2004), in a study of the performance of casework teams in a large state child welfare system in the USA, found that these 'political' skills of leaders explained a significant proportion of the variation in performance between teams.

Having said all that, self-directed teams are beginning to emerge in which a group of people have day-to-day responsibility for managing themselves and the work they do. Leadership tasks, for example setting direction or managing conflict, can be taken up by anyone in the group. As individuals accept more responsibility for their work, they also take on a stronger role in leading others. Increasingly in team-based organisations, team members also practise some degree of self-management, taking responsibility for the team outcomes by monitoring and managing their own performance, as well as helping others to improve their practice.

The learning organisation

The final piece in the jigsaw of managing increasing complexity involves recognising and developing the learning potential of whole organisations.

Managing change

Although a concern for social justice and the changes that necessarily accompany that goal have long been at the heart of social work practice and values, social workers frequently experience major difficulties when faced with change within their own organisations. While some of these difficulties can be attributed to the ways in which change has occurred, including the often limited extent to which social workers themselves have been involved in the planning, implementation and evaluation processes, others can perhaps be put down to a failure to apply the knowledge and skills that social workers routinely use in helping service users to cope with change. For example, although organisational change often occurs in response to factors external to the organisation, and social workers routinely consider the influence of the wider environment on the well-being of service users, this knowledge is not necessarily put to good use in coping with changes occurring in their own workplaces. The message here is that you are already likely to possess many of the skills needed to participate successfully in the management of organisational change. To take just one example, you will no doubt be aware from your own practice experience that it is pointless attempting to change the behaviour of individuals or groups unless they recognise and accept the need for change themselves. The same is true of organisations, sections or teams – the impetus for successful change must come from the within.

However, even when the need for change has been accepted, managing it will always have an emotional element. Handy (1993) developed a five stage model, set out in Figure 12.3, to chart the emotional impact of change.

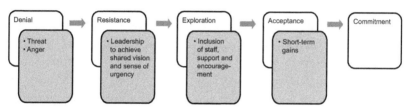

Figure 12.3 Five stage model of change management

The diagram represents the transition from initial feelings of threat and anger, which fuel resistance, through exploration and acceptance, to final commitment. Leadership is needed at each stage: to respond to feelings of threat; to achieve a shared vision; to consult with and include staff at every stage; and, to provide encouragement, support and a variety of short-term gains to secure final commitment.

It has been well documented that creating any form of change will meet with resistance, which may be rooted in a whole host of factors (Plant 1987):

Fear of the unknown	Lack of information or misinformation
Poor relationships	Lack of trust in the organisation
Threat to core skills	Threat to status
Threat to power base	No perceived benefits
Fear of failure	Reluctance to experiment
Strong fixed culture	Reluctance to let go

One of the most influential models of change (Lewin 1952) identifies a three-step process – unfreezing, moving and refreezing – in which unfreezing involves creating an awareness among stakeholders that change in a system is needed, and the possible methods of achieving it. Moving involves choosing one of the methods of change and putting it into action, and, after action has taken place, refreezing is required to consolidate and stabilise the new order.

Later, Lewin borrowed from Newton's third law of motion to develop a technique known as force field analysis, which can be used to evaluate organisational change. Newton demonstrated that 'for every action there is an equal and opposite reaction' which, translated into change management theory, means that the more you push for change, the more resistance you will meet. The solution proposed by Lewin (1952) was to stop pushing, and to seek out the cause of the impasse by listing all the forces that are supporting or driving the proposed change on the left-hand side of a piece of paper, and all the forces that are resisting or restraining the change on the right-hand side. You then look for ways in which the restraining forces can be reduced and the driving forces increased, in order to shift the equilibrium towards the proposed change.

Lewin's formulation of force field analysis tends to treat resistance as a single state, but other writers (e.g. Fink, Beak and Taddeo 1971) have identified different phases of resistance through which teams and organisations may pass in wrestling with their resistance to change, which we have represented in Figure 12.4.

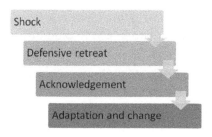

Figure 12.4 Phases of resistance to change

In the *shock* phase, relationships, decision-making and communication become confused and frozen, leading to *defensive retreat*. Teams and their members withdraw into a constrained mode of operation, characterised by rigidly applied procedures and autocratic decision-making. Once the need for things to change has been *acknowledged*, more confrontation is experienced but support also develops, so that, when the final stage – *adaptation and change* – is reached, communication is wider, more open and trusting, and a willingness to experiment creatively with different ways of working is adopted.

The message here is that just because you have worked through the options and devised what you think is a good solution, it does not follow that others will accept it without the opportunity to go through their own thinking processes, as noted by Hawkins and Shohet (2006):

> It can be counterproductive to give people your marvellous scenarios for their future. They need to be involved in the thinking through and planning changes so that they have the opportunity to react, then understand the need for change, and then adapt to the future necessities. (Hawkins and Shohet 2006, p.187)

Learning teams

Whereas in Chapter 11 we described culture as the social glue of organisations, there is a sense in which learning can be viewed as the 'professional glue' that is also essential for binding an organisation together.

No doubt part of your motivation for choosing a social work career was to have the opportunity to learn new things, acquire new skills and play a part in developing new knowledge. Using learning as a tool and central theme with which to bind disparate organisational units together is an idea drawn from ideas associated with the concept of the learning organisation. Gould (2000) has discussed ways in which these ideas, originally based in business management theory, might be translated into strategies for the development of social work practice by focusing on the team as the primary context for learning, which supports a reflective cycle of action that becomes part of everyday, professional activity. Teams have the potential to learn and recreate themselves, to set challenging new goals, and to be self-directive and reflective, thinking insightfully together about complex issues (Lick 2006). In this way, learning, training and development are not discrete activities, separate from practice, but rather fully integrated with it. We have seen that social workers place high value for their support and learning on members of their teams, as well as on more formal learning and development opportunities, and it would not be difficult for you to identify a number of team-based activities that could be translated into learning opportunities, including, for instance:

- presentations to team meetings
- sharing learning from external events
- co-working with colleagues
- joint working with internal and external partners
- sharing knowledge between teams
- workshops and seminars, and
- secondments across the agency and with partner organisations.

The Social Care Institute for Excellence (SCIE 2004) has identified five areas in which the characteristics of a learning organisation can be demonstrated, and it might be interesting for you to use the answers to the following questions to gauge the stage of development of your own agency as a learning organisation.

1. ORGANISATIONAL STRUCTURE

- *Service user and carer feedback and participation*: How well is this sought, resourced and used to inform practice?

- *Team working*: How well does your agency make use of different staff skills?

- *Collaboration*: How collaborative or 'parallel' is partnership working?

2. ORGANISATIONAL CULTURE

- *Shared vision*: How are beliefs, values, goals and objectives communicated?

- *Creativity*: Are new ideas and methods encouraged?

- *Learning*: Are you encouraged to learn from mistakes or test out new ideas?

- *Research*: Are messages and evidence from research considered and used in practice?

3. INFORMATION SYSTEMS

- *Effective information systems*: How effectively can you use systems for internal and external communication?

- *Policies and procedures*: How accessible, meaningful and understood are these?

4. HUMAN RESOURCE PRACTICES

- *Continuous development*: How clear are the supervision and appraisal policies?

5. LEADERSHIP

- *Organisational change and service development*: What capacity is there for development and change beyond day-to-day delivery?

Learning organisations challenge individuals to look at their own work and role more broadly, to develop their knowledge and skills for the benefit of all, rather than avoiding change, stagnating and taking refuge in a rut. The organisation that learns develops its own irresistible forward momentum in which the whole workforce has an investment.

Practitioner knowledge bank

Another important element from learning organisation theory which could enhance the workplace culture is the value accorded to the practice knowledge held by practitioners (Gould 2000), which is often unacknowledged. Recognising and recording its existence, actively building an agency knowledge bank and promoting it as a practice resource within and between teams, as well as with senior managers, could provide a further mechanism through which different elements of the organisation become networked, so that cohesion and communication, horizontally between peers and hierarchically between levels, is enhanced.

Key considerations in managing increasing complexity

Drawing on the work of Clarke and Stewart (1997), you might find the following suggestions helpful in developing a critically reflective response to problems that seem tricky and resistant to resolution.

- Instead of searching for certainty, try to accept that your understanding will be partial, and foster your ability to tolerate not knowing.

- Limiting yourself to thinking in a linear way might mean that you miss the important interrelationships that a more holistic approach can reveal.

- Accept different perspectives and approaches. You do not have to be constrained by the obvious or conventional, limiting your practice to 'the way things have always been done around here'.

- Draw on as wide an array of opinions and interests as possible, including being open to 'outsiders' and their new attitudes, ideas and perspectives.

- Spread your net as wide as possible, and consult not just the usual people with the usual answers. Be prepared to learn from experiment, innovation and creativity.

Additional Resources

England

Examples and templates for time and task-based models.
Organisations and Workloads – a Health Check – *Annex A: Final Report of Social Work Task Force* (2009): http://webarchive.nationalarchives.gov.uk/20131027134119/http://media.education.gov.uk/assets/files/pdf/social%20work%20task%20force%20health%20check.pdf.

Northern Ireland

A points-based system for all categories of child care practice.
Caseload Management Model, DHSSPS (2011): www.dhsspsni.gov.uk/oss-guide-rit–6–2011.pdf.

Scotland

A simple time-based template.
Supervision and Workload Management for Social Work, UNISON/BASW (2009): www.unison-scotland.org.uk/socialwork/workloadmanagement.pdf.

Wales

A practical tool intended to aid social workers in their practice and contribute to good outcomes for service users.
The Social Worker Practice Guidance, Care Council for Wales (2014): www.ccwales.org.uk/practice-guidance-for-social-workers.

References

ADSS (2005) *Social Work in Wales: A Profession to Value.* Cardiff, UK: ADSS Cymru.

Ahearn, K. K., Ferris, G. R., Hochwarter, W. A., Douglas, C. and Ammeter, A. P. (2004) 'Leader political skill and team performance.' *Journal of Management 30,* 3, 309–327.

APPG/BASW (2013) *Inquiry into the State of Social Work Report.* London, UK: All Party Parliamentary Group on Social Work/British Association of Social Workers.

Asquith, S. Clark, C. and Waterhouse, L. (2005) *The Role of the Social Worker in the 21st Century: A Literature Review.* Edinburgh, UK: The Scottish Executive.

Baginsky, M., Moriarty, J., Manthorpe, J., Stevens, M., MacInnes, T. and Nagndran, T. (2010) *Social Workers' Workload Survey: Messages for the Front Line. Findings from the 2009 Survey and Interviews with Senior Managers.* London, UK: Department for Children, Schools and Families.

Banks, S. (2002) 'Professional Values and Accountabilities.' In R. Adams, Dominelli, L. and Payne, M. (eds) *Critical Practice in Social Work.* London, UK: Palgrave Macmillan.

Barnett, R. (1997) *Higher Education: A Critical Business.* Buckingham, UK: Open University Press.

Beddoe, L., Davys, A. and Adamson, C. (2011) 'Educating resilient practitioners.' *Social Work Education 32,* 1, 100–117.

Bednar, S. G. (2003) 'Elements of satisfying organisational climates in child welfare agencies.' *Families in Society 84,* 1, 7–12.

Belbin, R. M. (2004) *Management Teams: Why They Succeed or Fail* (2nd edn). Oxford, UK: Elsevier Butterworth-Heinemann.

Bennett, P., Evans, R. and Tattersall, A. (1993) 'Stress and coping in social workers: A preliminary investigation.' *British Journal of Social Work 23,* 1, 31–44.

Beresford, P. (2012) 'What service users want from social workers.' *Community Care,* Adults Mental Health Workforce, 27 April 2012.

Berkowitz, A. D. and Perkins, H. W. (1984) 'Stress among farm women: Work and family as interacting systems.' *Journal of Marriage and the Family 46,* 1, 161–166.

Blewett, J., Lewis, J. and Tunstill, J. (2007) *The Changing Roles and Tasks of Social Work: A Literature Informed Discussion Paper.* London, UK: GSCC.

Bogues, S. (2008) *People Work Not Just Paperwork.* Belfast: Northern Ireland Social Care Council.

Brown, A. and Bourne, I. (1996) *The Social Work Supervisor.* Buckingham, UK: Open University Press.

Burton, N. W. and Turrell, G. (2000) 'Occupation, hours worked and leisure-time physical activity.' *Preventative Medicine 31,* 6, 673–681.

Carpenter, J., Patsios, D., Wood, M., Platt, D. *et al.* (2012) *Newly Qualified Social Worker Programme – Final Evaluation Report (2008–2011).* London, UK: Department for Education.

Carroll, M. and Gilbert, M. C. (2005) *On Being a Supervisee – Creating Learning Partnerships.* London, UK: Vukani Publishing.

CCW (2008) *Making the Most of the First Year in Practice: A Guide for Newly Qualified Social Workers.* Cardiff, UK: Care Council for Wales.

Charles, M. and Butler, S. (2004) 'Social Workers' Management of Organisational Change.' In M. Lymbery and S. Butler (eds) *Social Work Ideals and Practice Realities.* Basingstoke, UK: Palgrave Macmillan.

Clarke, M. and Stewart. J. (1997) *Handling the Wicked Issues: A Challenge for Government*. Birmingham, UK: Birmingham University School of Public Policy.

Collins, S. (2007) 'Social workers, resilience, positive emotions and optimism.' *Practice 19*, 4, 255–269.

Collins, S. (2008) 'Statutory social workers: Stress, job satisfaction, coping, social support and individual differences.' *British Journal Social Work 38*, 6, 1173–1193.

Community Care (2005) 'Profession becoming less focused on clients and more on paperwork.' *Community Care*, 15 December 2005.

Community Care (2008) 'GSCC's Mike Wardle calls for minimum client/worker ratio.' *Community Care*, 9 December 2008.

Corbett, D. (1991) *Public Sector Management*. Sydney, Australia: Allen and Unwin.

Croisdale-Appleby, D. (2014) *Re-Visioning Social Work Education: An Independent Review on the Education of Social Workers*. London, UK: Department of Health. Available at https://www.gov.uk/government/publications/social-work-education-review, accessed 8 October 2014.

CSCI (2006) *Supporting Parents, Safeguarding Children: Meeting the Needs of Parents with Children on the Child Protection Register*. London, UK: Commission for Social Care Inspection.

CWDC (2009) *Early Career Development: Guide for Supervisors*. Leeds, UK: Children's Workforce Development Council.

DCSF (2008) *Building Brighter Futures: Next Steps for the Children's Workforce*. Nottingham, UK: Department for Children, Schools and Families.

Dekel, R., Hantman, S., Ginzburg, K. and Solomon, Z. (2006) 'The cost of caring? Social workers in hospitals confront ongoing terrorism. *British Journal of Social Work 27*, 3, 1247–1261.

DfES (2003) *Raising Standards and Tackling Workload: a National Agreement. Time for Standards*. London, UK: Teacher Development Agency/Department for Education and Science.

DHSSPS (2012) *Social Work Strategy 2012–2022*. Belfast, UK: Department of Health, Social Services and Public Safety.

Dickens, J. (2012) 'The definition of social work in the United Kingdom, 2000–2010. *International Journal of Social Welfare 21*, 1, 34–43.

Dreyfus, H. and Dreyfus, S. (1986) *Mind Over Machine: The Power of Human Intuition and Expertise in the Era of the Computer*. Oxford, UK: Basil Blackwell.

Eraut, M. (1994) *Developing Professional Knowledge and Competence*. London, UK: Falmer Press.

Fineman, S. (1985) *Social Work Stress and Intervention*. Aldershot, UK: Gower.

Fink, S. C., Beak, J. and Taddeo, K. (1971) 'Organizational crisis and change.' *Journal of Applied Behavioural Science 17*, 1, 14–37.

Fook, J. and Gardner, F. (2007) *Practising Critical Reflection*. Maidenhead, UK: Open University Press/McGraw Hill Education.

Fook, J., Ryan, M. and Hawkins, L. (2000) *Professional Expertise: Practice, Theory and Education for Working in Uncertainty*. London, UK: Whiting and Birch.

French, R. (2001) 'Negative capability: Managing the confusing uncertainties of change.' *Journal of Organizational Change Management 14*, 5, 480–492.

GSCC (2008) *Social Work at its Best: A Statement of Social Work Roles and Tasks for the 21st Century*. London, UK: General Social Care Council.

GSCC (2013) *Regulating Social Workers 2001–2012*. London, UK: General Social Care Council.

Gerrish, K. (2005) 'Still fumbling along? A comparative study of newly qualified nurses' perception of the transition from student to qualified nurse.' *Journal of Advanced Nursing 32*, 2, 473–480.

Glisson, C. and Hemmelgarn, A. (1998) 'The effects of organizational climate and inter-organizational coordination on the quality and outcomes of children's service systems.' *Child Abuse and Neglect 22*, 5, 401–421.

Gould, N. (2000) 'Becoming a learning organisation: A social work example.' *Social Work Education 19*, 6, 585–596.

Gould, N. and Baldwin, M. (2004) *Social Work, Critical Reflection and the Learning Organisation*. Aldershot, UK: Ashgate.

Grant, L. and Kinman, G. (2012) 'Enhancing wellbeing in social work students: Building resilience in the next generation.' *Social Work Education 31*, 5, 605–621.

Guerin, S., Devitt, C. and Redmond, B. (2010) 'Experiences of early-career social workers in Ireland.' *British Journal of Social Work 40*, 8, 2467–2484.

Handy, C. (1993) *Understanding Organisations*. Harmondsworth, UK: Penguin.

Harrison, R. (1972) 'Understanding your organisation's character.' *Harvard Business Review, May–June*, 119–128.

Hawkins, P. and Shohet, R. (2006) *Supervision in the Helping Professions* (3rd edn). Buckingham, UK: Open University Press.

HCPC (2012a) 'Social work student suitability scheme in England.' Available at www.hpc-uk.org/education/studentsuitability, accessed on 9 September 2014.

HCPC (2012b) 'Standards of proficiency: Social workers in England.' Available at www.hpc-uk.org/publications/standards/index.asp?id=569, accessed on 9 September 2014.

Heron, J. (1975) *Six-Category Intervention Analysis*. Guildford, UK: University of Surrey Human Potential Research Project.

Hughes, L. and Pengelly, P. (1997) *Staff Supervision in a Turbulent Environment: Managing Process and Task in Front-Line Services*. London, UK: Jessica Kingsley Publishers.

Hughes, M. and Wearing, M. (2007) *Organisations and Management in Social Work*. London, UK: Sage Publications.

IFSW (2014) 'Global definition of social work: Proposal for approval in July 2014.' Available at http://ifsw.org/get-involved/global-definition-of-social-work, accessed on 9 September 2014.

Jenaro, C., Flores, N. and Arias, B. (2007) 'Burnout and coping in human service practitioners.' *Professional Psychology: Research and Practice 38*, 1, 80–87.

Jimmieson, N. L. (2000) 'Employee reactions to behavioural control under conditions of stress: The moderating role of self-efficacy.' *Work and Stress 14*, 3, 262–280.

Johns, C. (1994) 'Guided Reflection.' In A. Palmer, S. Burns and C. Bulman (eds) *Reflective Practice in Nursing*. Chichester, UK: Blackwell Scientific Publishers.

Jones, C. (2001) 'Voices from the front line: State social workers and New Labour.' *British Journal of Social Work 31*, 4, 547–562.

Jones, F., Fletcher, B. E. N. and Ibbetson, K. (1991) 'Stressors and strains amongst social workers: Demands, supports, constraints, and psychological health.' *British Journal of Social Work 21*, 5, 443–469.

JRF (2011) 'Transforming Social Care: Sustaining Person-Centred Support' *Findings: Informing Change*. York, UK: Standards We Expect Consortium/Joseph Rowntree Foundation.

Kadushin, A. (1976) *Supervision in Social Work*. New York, NY: Columbia University Press.

Karasek, R. A. (1979) 'Job demands, job decision latitude and mental strain: Implications for job redesign.' *Administrative Science Quarterly 24*, 285–308.

Kirschbaum, C., Klauer, T., Filipp, S. H. and Hellhammer, D. H. (1995) 'Sex-specific effects of social support on cortisol and subjective responses to acute psychological stress.' *Psychosomatic Medicine 57*, 1, 23–31.

Kolb, D. (1984) *Experiential Learning*. Englewood Cliffs, NJ: Prentice-Hall.

Kouvonen, A., Kivimäki, M., Elovainio, M., Virtanen, M., Linna, A. and Vahtera, J. (2005) 'Job strain and leisure-time physical activity in female and male public sector employees.' *Preventive Medicine 41*, 2, 532–539.

Kramer, M. (1974) *Reality Shock: Why Nurses Leave Nursing*. Saint Louis, MO: The CV Mosby Company.

Lacey, C. (1977) *The Socialisation of Teachers*. London, UK: Methuen.

Lazarus, R. S. and Folkman, S. (1984) *Stress, Appraisal and Coping*. New York, NY: Springer.

Lens, V. (2004) 'Principled negotiation: A new tool for case advocacy.' *Social Work 49*, 3, 506–513.

Lepore, S. J., Ragan, J. D. and Jones, S. (2000) 'Talking facilitates cognitive emotional processes of adaptation to an acute stressor.' *Journal of Personality and Social Psychology 78*, 3, 499–508.

Lewin, K. (1952) *Field Theory in Social Science*. New York, NY: Harper and Row.

LGA (2014) *Standards for Employers of Social Workers in England and Supervision Framework.* London, UK: Local Government Association/Social Work Reform Board. Available at www.local.gov.uk/documents/10180/6188796/The_standards_for_employers_of_social_workers.pdf/fb7cb809-650c-4ccd-8aa7-fecb072711c4a, accessed on 8 October 8 2014.

Lick, D. W. (2006) 'A new perspective on organizational learning: Creating learning teams.' *Evaluation and Program Planning 29*, 1, 88–96.

Lodge, G. and Schmuecker, K. (2012) *Devolution in Practice III: Public Policy Differences in the UK.* Newcastle, UK: IPPR North.

Lysons, K. (1997) 'Organisational analysis.' *British Journal of Administrative Management,* 16 March.

Maben, J. and Macleod Clark, J. (1998) 'Project 2000 diplomates' perceptions of experiences of transition from student to staff nurse.' *Journal of Clinical Nursing 7*, 2, 145–153.

McGee, R. A. (1989) 'Burnout and professional decision making: An analogue study.' *Journal of Counseling Psychology 36*, 3, 345–351.

Martin, R. A. (2001) 'Humor, laughter, and physical health: Methodological issues and research findings.' *Psychological Bulletin 127*, 4, 504–519.

Maslach, C. (1980) *Burnout: The Cost of Caring.* Englewood Cliffs, NJ: Prentice Hall.

Maslach, C. and Leiter, M. P. (1997) *The Truth about Burnout: How Organisations Cause Personal Stress and What to Do about It.* San Francisco, CA: Jossey-Bass Wiley.

Maslow, A. H. (1943) 'A Theory of Human Motivation.' *Psychological Review 50*, 4, 370–396.

Mattinson, J. (1981) 'The Deadly Equal Triangle.' In *Change and Renewal in Psychodynamic Social Work: British and American Developments in Practice and Education for Services in Families and Children.* Northampton, MA: Smith College School of Social Work.

Michie, S. and Cockcroft, A. (1996) 'Overwork can kill.' *British Medical Journal 312*, 7036, 921–922.

Middleman, R. and Rhodes, G. (1980) 'Teaching the practice of supervision.' *Journal of Education for Social Work 16*, 3, 51–59.

Mooney, M. (2007) 'Newly qualified Irish nurses' interpretation of their preparation and experiences of registration.' *Journal of Clinical Nursing 16*, 9, 1610–1617.

Moran, C. C. and Hughes, L. P. (2006) 'Coping with stress: Social work students and humour.' *Social Work Education 25*, 5, 501–517.

Morgan, R. (2006) *About Social Workers: A Children's Views Report.* Newcastle: Commission for Social Care Inspectorate.

Morris, L. (2005) 'The process of decision-making by stressed social workers: To stay or leave the workplace.' *International Review of Psychiatry 17*, 5, 347–354.

Morrison, T. (2001) *Staff Supervision in Social Care: Making a Real Difference for Staff and Service Users.* Brighton, UK: Pavilion.

Morrison, T. and Wonnacott, J. (2010) 'Supervision Now or Never: Reclaiming Reflective Supervision in Social Work.' Available at www.in-trac.co.uk/supervision-now-or-never, accessed on 9 September 2014.

Nellis, M. (2001) 'The Diploma in Probation Studies in the Midland region: Celebration and critique after the first two years.' *The Howard Journal of Criminal Justice 40*, 4, 377–401.

Noakes, S., Hearn, B., Burton, S. and Wonnacott, J. (1998) *Developing Good Child Protection Practice: A Guide for First Line Managers.* London, UK: National Children's Bureau.

NISCC (2010) *The Assessed Year in Employment: Guidance for Registrants and Employers.* Belfast, UK: Northern Ireland Social Care Council.

NISSC (2013) *Readiness to Practise: A Report from a Study of New Social Work Graduates' Preparedness for Practice: An Analysis of the Views of Key Stakeholders.* Belfast, UK: Northern Ireland Social Care Council.

Parkinson, J. and Pritchard, J. (2005) 'The induction experiences of newly-qualified secondary teachers in England and Wales.' *Journal of In-Service Education 31*, 1, 63–81.

Pearson, G. (1973) 'Social work as the privatized solution of public ills.' *British Journal of Social Work 3*, 2, 209–227.

Plant, R. (1987) *Managing Change and Making it Stick.* London, UK: Fontana.

QAA (2008) 'Benchmark statements for social work.' Gloucester, UK: The Quality Assurance Agency for Higher Education. Available at www.qaa.ac.uk/en/Publications/Documents/Subject-benchmark-statement-Social-work.pdf, accessed on 8 October 2014.

Rautkis, M. E. and Koeske, G. F. (1994) 'Maintaining social worker morale: When supportive supervision is not enough.' *Administration in Social Work 18*, 1, 39–60.

Roberts, A. R. (2000) *Crisis Intervention Handbook: Assessment, Treatment and Research* (2nd edn). Oxford, UK: Oxford University Press.

Robinson, V. (1936) *Supervision in Social Casework: A Problem in Professional Education.* Chapel Hill, NC: University of North Carolina Press.

SCIE (2004) 'Learning Organisations: A Self-Assessment Resource Pack – Key Characteristics.' Available at www.scie.org.uk/publications/learningorgs/files/key_characteristics_2.pdf, accessed on 9 September 2014.

SCIE (2012) 'Research Briefing 43: Effective Supervision in Social Work and Social Care.' London, UK: Social Care Institute for Excellence. Available at www.scie.org.uk/publications/briefings/briefing43, accessed on 9 September 2014.

Scottish Government (2011) *Practice Governance Framework: Responsibility and Accountability in Social Work Practice.* Edinburgh, UK: Scottish Government.

SCWRU (2008) *Evaluation of the New Social Work Degree Qualification in England: Volume 1: Findings.* London, UK: University of London. King's College. Social Care Workforce Research Unit.

Schön, D. (1983) *The Reflective Practitioner.* New York, NY: Basic Books.

Scottish Executive (2002) *Action Plan for the Social Services Workforce.* Edinburgh, UK: Scottish Executive.

Scottish Executive (2006a) *Changing Lives: Report of the 21st Century Social Work Review.* Edinburgh, UK: Scottish Executive.

Scottish Executive (2006b) *Key Capabilities in Child Care and Child Protection.* Edinburgh, UK: Scottish Executive.

Scottish Government (2003) *Standards in Social Work Education (SiSWE).* Edinburgh, UK: Scottish Government.

Seebohm, F. (1968) *Report of the Committee on Local Authority and Allied Personal Social Services (the Seebohm Report).* London, UK: HMSO.

Seligman, M. (1975) *Learned Helplessness.* San Francisco, CA: Freeman.

Seligman, M. (2006) *Learned Optimism: How to Change your Mind and your Life.* New York, NY: Vintage Books.

SfC (2013) *Developing Social Workers' Practice: Core Principles for Employers Providing Opportunities for Social Workers' Continuing Professional Development.* Leeds, UK: Skills for Care.

Shulman, L. (1982) *Skills of Supervision and Staff Management.* Itasca, IL: F.E. Peacock Publishers Inc.

Siviter, B. (2008) *The Newly-Qualified Nurses' Handbook: A Survival Guide.* London, UK: Bailliere Tindall, Elsevier.

Smith, M. and Nursten, J. (1998) 'Social workers' experience of distress: Moving towards change?' *British Journal of Social Work 28*, 3, 351–368.

Smith, R., McLenachan, J., Venn, L., Weich, H., Anthony, D. and DeMontfort University (2013) 'Step up to social work programme evaluation 2012: The regional partnerships' and employers' perspectives'. London, UK: Department for Education. Available at www.gov.uk/government/uploads/system/uploads/attachment_data/file/205617/DFE-RR290.pdf, accessed on 6 October 2014.

Stalker, C. A., Mandell, D., Frensch, J. M., Harvey, C. and Wright, M. (2007) 'Child welfare workers who are exhausted yet satisfied with their jobs: How do they do it?' *Child and Family Social Work 12*, 2, 182–191.

Statham, J., Cameron, C. and Mooney, A. (2006) *The Tasks and Roles of Social Workers: A Focused Overview of Research Evidence.* London, UK: Thomas Coram Research Institute.

Stevenson, O. (1981) *Specialisation in Social Service Teams.* London, UK: George Allen and Unwin.

Storey, J. and Billingham, J. (2001) 'Occupational stress and social work.' *Social Work Education 20*, 6, 659–670.

SWRB (2010) *Building a Safe and Confident Future: One Year On*. London, UK: Social Work Reform Board.

SWRB (2012) *Building a Safe and Confident Future: Maintaining Momentum*. London, UK: Social Work Reform Board.

SWTF (2009a) *Building a Safe, Confident Future: Final Report of the Social Work Task Force, November 2009*. London, UK: Social Work Task Force.

SWTF (2009b) *Organisations and Workloads: A Health Check, Annex A of Final Report – Building a Safe and Confident Future*. London: Social Work Task Force. Available at http://dera.ioe.ac.uk/1910/1/SWTF%20Health%20Check%20(final).pdf, accessed on 8 October 2014.

Takeda, F., Ibaraki, N., Yokoyama, E., Miyake, T. and Ohida, T. (2005) 'The relationship of job type to burnout in social workers at social welfare offices.' *Journal of Occupational Therapy 47*, 2, 119–125.

Taylor, I. and Bogo, M. (2013) 'Perfect opportunity – perfect storm? Raising the standards of social work education in England.' *British Journal of Social Work*, accepted for publication February 2013; first published online 2 May 2013. doi: 10.1093/bjsw/bct077.

Taylor, S. E., Klein, L. C., Lewis, B. P., Gruenewald, T. L., Gurung, R. A. R. and Updegraff, J. A. (2000) 'Biobehavioral responses to stress in females: Tend-and-befriend, not fight-or-flight.' *Psychological Review 107*, 3, 411–429.

The College of Social Work (TCSW) (2010) *ASYE Level Capabilities*. Available at www.tcsw.org.uk/uploadedFiles/PCF10NOVASYELevel%20Capabilities.pdf, accessed 9 September 2014.

TCSW (2012) 'Capabilities rather than competences'. London, UK: TCSW. Available at www.tcsw.org.uk/professional-development/educators, accessed on 6 October 2014.

TCSW (2014) *Roles and Functions of Social Workers in England: Advice Note*. London, UK: The College of Social Work.

Thody, A., Gray, B., and Bowden, D. (2007) *The Teacher's Survival Guide* (2nd edn). London/New York: Continuum.

Thompson, N., Stradling, S., Murphy, M. and O'Neill, P. (1996) 'Stress and organizational culture.' *British Journal of Social Work 26*, 5, 647–665.

Tickle, L. (1994) *The Induction of New Teachers: Reflective Professional Practice*. London, UK: Cassell.

Topss UK Partnership. (2002) *The National Occupational Standards for Social Work*. Leeds, UK: Topss/Skills for Care.

TUC (2006) *Biennial Safety Survey of Representatives*. 30 October 2006. Available at www.tuc.org.uk/workplace-issues/health-and-safety/safety-representatives/stress/stress-still-biggest-problem-uk, accessed on 9 September 2014.

Tuckman, B. W. (1965) 'Developmental sequence in small groups.' *Psychological Bulletin 63*, 6, 384–399.

Warren, C. (1993) *Family Centres and the Children Act 1989*. Arundel, UK: Tarrant Publishing Ltd.

Welsh Assembly Government (2007) *Fulfilled Lives, Supported Communities*. Cardiff, UK: Welsh Assembly Government

Wharton, A. S. and Erickson, R. J. (1995) 'The consequences of caring: Exploring the links between women's jobs and family emotional work.' *Sociological Quarterly 36*, 2, 273–296.

Wrzesniewski, A. and Dutton, J. E. (2001) 'Crafting a job: Revisioning employees as active crafters of their work.' *Academy of Management Review 26*, 2, 179–201.

Yelloly, M. and Henkel, M. (eds) (1995) *Learning and Teaching in Social Work: Towards Reflective Practice*. London, UK: Jessica Kingsley Publishers.

Ying, Y.-W. (2008) 'The buffering effect of self-detachment against emotional exhaustion among social work students.' *Journal of Religion and Spirituality in Social Work: Social Thought 27*, 1, 127–146.

Subject Index

Author Index